Pandolfini Chess Library

Let's Play Chess

by

Bruce Pandolfini

2nd Edition
Revised and Enlarged

2009
Russell Enterprises, Inc.
Milford, CT USA

Let's Play Chess
2nd Edition

© Copyright 2009

Bruce Pandolfini

All Rights Reserved. No part of this book may be used, reproduced, stored in a retrieval system or transmitted in any manner or form whatsoever or by any means, electronic, electrostatic, magnetic tape, photocopying, recording or otherwise, without the express written permission from the publisher except in the case of brief quotations embodied in critical articles or reviews.

ISBN: 978-1-888690-52-1

Published by:
Russell Enterprises, Inc.
PO Box 5460
Milford, CT 06460 USA

http://www.chesscafe.com
info@chesscafe.com

Cover design by Janel Lowrance

Editing and Proofreading: Hanon Russell and Mark Donlan
Production: Mark Donlan

Printed in the United States of America

Table of Contents

Introduction

Chess is by far the most popular board game in the world. There are millions of players of all ages and the number keeps growing. This is my attempt to lure you to a challenging and fascinating pastime. It's based on the very same lessons I have given to thousands of beginners. Their questions and problems have shaped it. Moreover, some of the best ideas in the book were actually suggested by new players!

I have tried to be as plain and uncomplicated as possible. Just as certain individual problems are made simpler by partitioning them, I saw a correspondence with learning chess itself. Thus to make your journey a smoother one the fundamentals have been broken down into short, logical statements. Each idea is numbered, ordered, and clearly stated. In most sections statements are linked in graded sequence, with the easier ones preceding the harder. Yet this design is sometimes abandoned for elucidation or aptness. I hope you find the format simple enough to follow and the occasional digressions engaging and clarifying. If the overall approach works you should feel yourself learning step by step.

Throughout I have aimed to show how chess players think about their moves. All the ideas are expressed in words, so you don't have to struggle with variations of chess notation before seeing where a thought is going. Explanation has taken precedence over calculation, and the stress has been placed on understanding, not memory. There are also plenty of diagrams for almost every idea to provide visual reinforcement. So you should be able to read this book even without a chess set, though you might want to get one anyway. I hear they're useful for play and study. But then you don't really need a physical chess set in today's computer world of software and the Internet. It's all there, on the electronic highway, with access to thousands of sites and zillions of potential players.

How should you use *Let's Play Chess*? To get the most from your efforts, start with the first statement and begin reading in numbered order. Try to cover entire sections in one reading. If a particular point seems confusing don't get bogged down. Just read on. You can always come back after you've thought about it and learned more. Besides, you should be able to read this book and play chess without understanding every single detail right away. And that's one of the charms of chess. Whether you play at the elementary level, with command over almost nothing, or at the top echelon, as an exponent of the game's greatest principles, it's hard not to lose yourself in an engaging and compelling miniature universe. But that you can judge for yourself starting with statement number one.

Bruce Pandolfini
New York, New York
January 2009

Acknowledgments

I've had enough practice at this and still don't know how to do it. Unquestionably without the efforts of certain people *Let's Play Chess* wouldn't exist, and if it could exist without them it would be something else and something less. For their suggestions and creative work on the first edition I'd like to thank Roselyn Abrahams, Carol Ann Caronia, Bob Hernandez, Paul Hoffman, Idelle Pandolfini, and Iris Rosoff. I'd mention Ludwig Wittgenstein, but that would be a stretch. For their invaluable work on the second edition my appreciation goes to Mark Donlan, who painstakingly set and designed the present text and layout, and Hanon Russell, whose astute editing and thoughtful insights have fueled, guided, and overseen the entire second edition. While all of these able and talented people have improved my effort with their special stamp, the deficiencies in *Let's Play Chess* are entirely mine. Everything else must be passed over in silence.

Section One: General Rules

1. Chess is a game of skill played by two people on a board of sixty-four squares. The board is the same one used for checkers.

2. The squares of the chessboard are alternately colored light and dark and that helps the players see better.

Black

8	a8	b8	c8	d8	e8	f8	g8	h8
7	a7	b7	c7	d7	e7	f7	g7	h7
6	a6	b6	c6	d6	e6	f6	g6	h6
5	a5	b5	c5	d5	e5	f5	g5	h5
4	a4	b4	c4	d4	e4	f4	g4	h4
3	a3	b3	c3	d3	e3	f3	g3	h3
2	a2	b2	c2	d2	e2	f2	g2	h2
1	a1	b1	c1	d1	e1	f1	g1	h1
	a	b	c	d	e	f	g	h

White

3. The players, starting at opposite ends of the board, take turns by moving their own armies, one soldier on a turn.

4. Each army or side consists of sixteen soldiers. In common parlance these forces are referred to as "the pieces."

5. Indeed, a chess set is ordinarily said to have a "board and pieces." Yet chess players prefer to distinguish between pieces and pawns for a variety of practical reasons.

6. So herein **unit** will be used to mean either an individual **piece** or **pawn**.

7. All the forces constitute an element of the game known as **material**.

8. The lighter color material or side is always called **White** and the darker one **Black**, regardless of their actual colors.

9. The players take turns to move. White moves first, then Black, then White, then Black, and so on.

10. Turns are taken by moving or capturing.

11. A **move** is the transfer of a unit from one square to another.

12. Units are placed in the middle of squares and not on their intersections, as stones are in the game of *go*.

13. A move can be legal or illegal.

14. A **legal move** abides by the rules of the game: it can be played. An **illegal move** violates the rules of the game: it can't be played.

15. Illegal moves must be taken back and replayed.

16. A **capture** is a move that eliminates an opponent's unit from the board.

17. Individual units are not jumped, as checkers are in the game of checkers or draughts. Rather they are replaced by the capturing chess unit and removed.

18. Unlike checkers, in chess you are not forced to capture opposing forces. Instead it's a matter of choice, unless the situation requires that an opponent's particular unit be captured (for instance, if it's touched or if no other legal move is possible).

19. Any piece or pawn may capture any enemy unit provided it's a legal move.

20. No move or capture has to be played unless it's the only way to save the king from checkmate or if there's a touch-move infraction (more on both later).

21. You can't:
    (a) capture your own forces;
    (b) place two of your own units on the same square;
    (c) move two of your own units on a separate turn (except in the act of castling, which will be explained later);
    (d) capture more than one of your opponent's units on a single turn;
    (e) move a unit in two different directions on the same turn (except for the knight, which is yet to be explained).

Section Two: The Board, The Forces, and Their Names

22. The chessboard is the battlefield on which the two generals – you and your opponent – meet. It's a large square made up of sixty-four smaller squares (there are eight rows of eight squares each).

23. The smaller squares are arranged in three different kinds of rows:

   (a) horizontal rows
   (b) vertical rows
   (c) slanted rows

24. The horizontal rows are **ranks**, the vertical rows are **files**, and the slanted rows of one color are **diagonals**.

25. To explain the game of chess it's helpful to use diagrams. A diagram is a picture of a chess position in which symbols are used to represent the forces. For example, Diagram 2 illustrates the opening position of a chess game.

26. For all diagrams in this book White sits at the bottom and Black at the top. Consequently, the white pawns move up the board and the black move down. (See Diagram 3 at the top of the next page.)

Diagram 1
The chessboard

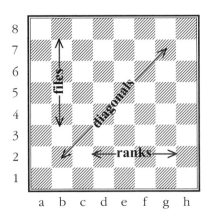

Diagram 2
The starting position
Black

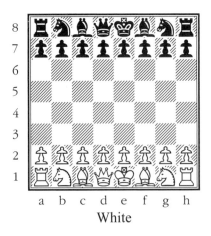

White

27. For both diagrams and real chess games each player must have a light square in the corner to his or her right.

28. Remember: **light on the right**.

29. Both you and your opponent start with an army of sixteen units, eight pieces and eight pawns each.

30. Each player has one king, one queen, two rooks, two bishops, two knights, and eight pawns.

31. The abbreviations for these units are: **K** for king; **Q** for queen; **R** for rook; **B** for bishop; **N** for knight; and **P** for pawn. Note that the knight is abbreviated with an N to avoid confusion with the abbreviation for king.

32. As a reminder, individual units are referred to as pieces or pawns. You may call any unit a piece that isn't a pawn.

33. At the start your pieces occupy the rank closest to you and your pawns occupy the next rank in.

34. From opposite sides of the starting setup the same kinds of white and black pieces occupy squares directly across from each other. Along the same files, rooks oppose rooks, knights oppose knights, and so on.

35. In setting up the pieces you might confuse the squares occupied by the queen and king. There's an easy way to avoid this confusion: queens always start on squares of their own color.

36. At the start White's queen occupies a light square and Black's a dark one (this is true only if you've set up correctly, with a light square in the corner to your right).

Diagram 3
Black's pawns move down the diagram

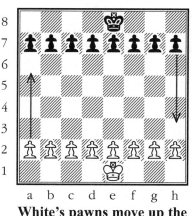

White's pawns move up the diagram

Diagram 4
The same kinds of pieces face each other at the start

37. Remember: **queen on the square of her own color**.

38. Each square, line and unit has a specific name. Once you've become more familiar with these names it becomes easier to talk about the game and its play without having to move the pieces.

39. Get into the habit of trying to see moves in your mind while minimizing the need to see them played on the board. That's one of the fastest ways to improve. If you can't "see ahead" it's hard to play chess with logic and purpose.

40. The board is divided in half into the **kingside** and **queenside**.

41. The rooks, bishops, and knights are named according to which side of the board they are on at the start of the game. Moving across the board from White's left to right, there's the queen-rook, the queen-knight, the queen-bishop, the queen, the king, the king-bishop, the king-knight, and the king-rook.

42. The name of a piece never changes, no matter where it's moved. The king-rook is always the king-rook even if it winds up on the queenside. Yet in case you can't say or remember which piece is which, there are other ways to tell the pieces and pawns apart based on the squares they occupy, as we shall soon see.

Diagram 5

The black queen occupies a dark square

The white queen occupies a light square.

Diagram 6

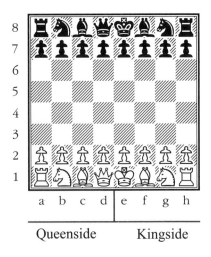

Queenside   Kingside

43. Files are named by the letters *a* through *h*. Starting from White's left and going toward the right, there's *the a-file, the b-file, the c-file,* and so on. At the start, kings occupy the e-file and queens the d-file.

44. The name of a file never changes, with both players using White's perspective. Thus the a-file is on White's left and Black's right.

45. Ranks are numbered *1* through *8* starting from White's side of the board.

46. Proceeding from White's side of the board and moving toward Black's there's the first rank, the second rank, the third rank, and so on.

47. At the start of play White's forces occupy the first and second ranks while Black's occupy the seventh and eighth ranks.

48. To name a square combine the letter of the file with the number of its intersecting rank. Every square therefore has but one name, regardless whose move it is. Both players name squares from White's point of view.

49. The illustration at right names the squares. For each name the lowercase letter always precedes the number.

50. Pawns take their names from the files they occupy at any given time. A pawn on the a-file is an *a-pawn*. (See Diagram 9 at the top of the next page.)

51. If two or more friendly pawns wind up appearing on the same file

Diagram 7

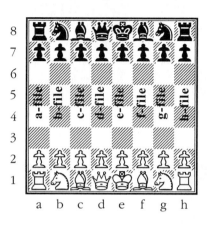

Diagram 8

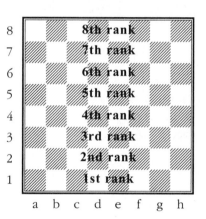

11

(by virtue of a capture), their naming is further distinguished by the number of the intersecting rank. Thus, if White has pawns on a2 and a3, the one on a2 is the a2-pawn and the one on a3 is the a3-pawn.

52. Groups of squares can be referred to by their color. Regardless of their actual colors the thirty-two darker squares are called **the dark squares** and the thirty-two lighter squares are called **the light squares**.

Diagram 9

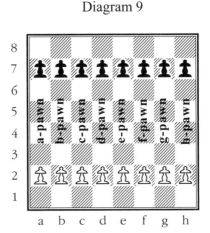

53. To tell apart better it's helpful to refer to squares as being *light* or *dark* and pieces and pawns as being *white* or *black*. Moreover, when signifying the player, *White* and *Black* are capitalized. When referring to the color of the pieces and pawns, *white* and *black* should be lowercase.

54. Now you should be able to refer to any part of the board or kind of chess unit with accuracy. But there's a lot more to know. I just haven't told you yet.

Section Three: The Moves of the Pieces

The King

55. The **king** is usually the tallest and always the most important piece, though its significance won't be clear until a little later.

56. The king moves just one square at a time in any direction.

57. In Diagram 10 the king can move to any square marked by a star.

58. The king captures by moving as it would normally and then replacing the opposing piece or pawn occupying the square to which it transfers.

59. In Diagrams 11 and 12 the white king captures the black knight (on the first move it could also capture the black pawn, but not the black rook).

Diagram 10
The king's move

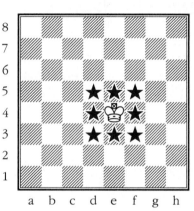

To any square marked by a dot

Diagram 11
Before

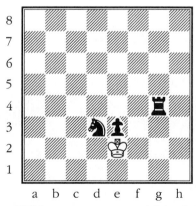

White may capture either the knight or pawn

Diagram 12
After

White has captured the knight

13

60. Kings can't:

    (a) take their own pieces or pawns;

    (b) move to squares occupied by their own forces;

    (c) jump over enemy or friendly pieces or pawns;

    (d) capture two or more enemy units on the same turn;

    (e) move where they could be captured (more on this shortly).

The Rook

61. The **rook** is the piece colloquially called the castle.

62. The rook moves along ranks and files (forward, backward, or sideways) as many unblocked squares as desired.

63. The rook can move in only one direction on a turn (whichever one you choose).

64. In Diagram 13 the rook can move to any square marked by a star.

Diagram 13
The rook's move

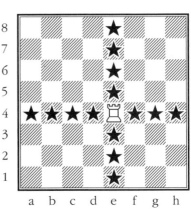

To any square marked by a star

65. A rook captures by moving in its normal way and then replacing the enemy piece or pawn occupying the square to which it transfers.

66. In Diagrams 14 and 15 the rook captures the bishop (it could also have captured the knight).

67. Rooks can't:

    (a) take their own pieces or pawns;

    (b) move to squares occupied by their own forces;

    (c) jump over opposing or friendly pieces or pawns;

    (d) capture two or more opposing units on the same turn;

    (e) move diagonally;

    (f) move or capture in two different directions on the same turn.

The Bishop

68. The **bishop** moves only on diagonals (the slanted rows of one color) as many unblocked squares as desired.

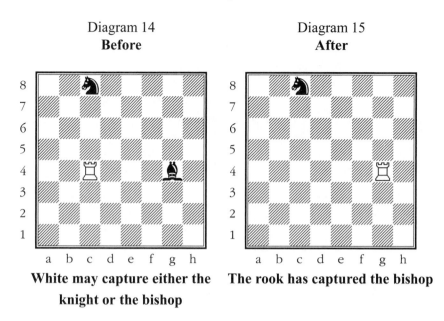

Diagram 14
Before

Diagram 15
After

White may capture either the knight or the bishop

The rook has captured the bishop

69. Bishops move diagonally backward or forward, but only in one direction on a turn.

70. In Diagram 16 the bishop can move to any square marked by a star.

71. A bishop captures by moving in its normal way and then replacing the opposing unit occupying the square to which it transfers.

72. Each side starts with both a light-squared and a dark-squared bishop. A **light-squared bishop** travels only on light squares, while the **dark-squared bishop** travels only on dark squares (this is determined by the color of the square the bishop occupies at the start of the game).

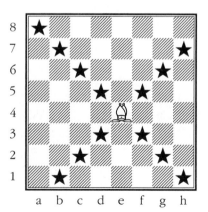

Diagram 16
The bishop's move

To any square marked by a star

73. Bishops can't:
 (a) capture two or more opposing units on a turn;
 (b) capture their own pieces
 and pawns;

(c) jump over opposing or friendly pieces and pawns;

(d) move to a square occupied by one of their own units;

(e) move along ranks and files;

(f) move or capture in two different directions on the same turn.

74. In Diagrams 17 and 18 the bishop captures the rook.

Diagram 17   Diagram 18

Before   **After**

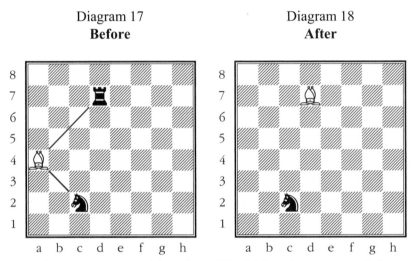

White may capture either the   **The bishop has captured the rook**

rook or the knight

75. How many moves would it take for a bishop starting on c8 to reach a3?

76. Answer: none. It can't be done! A light-squared bishop can never move to a dark square (nor can a dark-squared bishop move to a light square).

77. During the course of a game a bishop can occupy no more than thirty-two different squares on the board. Compare this to a rook, which is capable of reaching every square, all sixty-four of them. Do the math.

Diagram 19

Can the bishop reach a3?

The Queen

78. The **queen** is the most powerful piece of all, though not the most important. That honor is held by the king.

79. The queen combines the movements of the rook and bishop. This means that for any move it functions as both rook and bishop, being able to move along files, ranks, and diagonals.

80. With all the queen's powers it still can move in only one direction on a turn (forward, backward, sideways, or diagonally) as many unblocked squares as desired.

81. In Diagram 20 the queen can move to any square marked by a star.

Diagram 20
The queen's move

To any square marked by a star

82. The queen captures by moving in its normal way and then replacing the opposing unit occupying the square to which it transfers.

Diagram 21
Before

Diagram 22
After

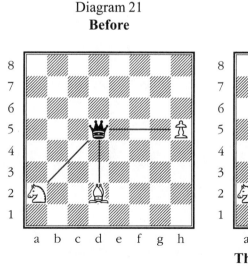

The queen has captured the bishop

83. In Diagram 21 the queen has the option of capturing any of the three opposing units, but only one of them on the next turn. Diagram 22 shows the queen having captured the bishop.

84. The queen can't:
(a) capture its own units;
(b) jump over opposing or friendly chess units;
(c) move to a square occupied by one of its own pieces or pawns;
(d) capture two or more opposing units on the same turn;
(e) move or capture in two different directions on the same turn.

The Knight

85. The **knight** is the piece colloquially called the horse.

86. Its movement is the most difficult to learn because in some descriptions it has two different parts. Both parts together, however, are to be viewed as one complete turn.

87. The knight can move in any direction, but it must always make a move of the same length.

88. The knight's move looks like the capital letter **L**.

89. Before describing it further let's examine it. In Diagram 23 the knight can move to any square marked by a star. Notice that the stars seem to form a circle around the knight.

90. There are various ways to describe the knight's movement. We shall examine four of them.

91. The knight can move:
(a) two squares vertically then one square horizontally;
(b) one square horizontally then two squares vertically;
(c) two squares horizontally then one square vertically;

Diagram 23
The knight's move

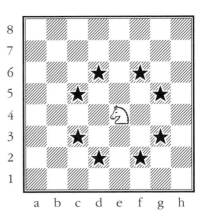

To any square marked by a star

18

(d) one square vertically then two squares horizontally.

Diagrams 24 and 25 show the same knight moves:

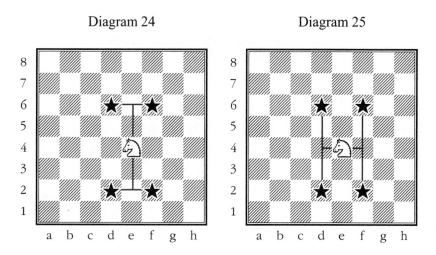

Diagram 24   Diagram 25

Diagrams 26 and 27 show the same knight moves:

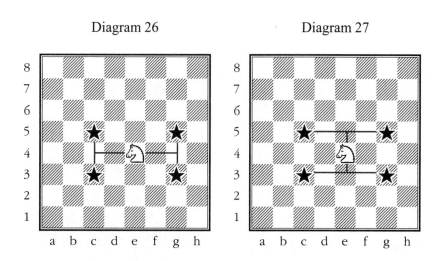

Diagram 26   Diagram 27

92. Notice that 91a and 91b describe one set of knight moves, while 91c and 91d describe another set of knight moves.

93. Thus, by the system in 91a-d, each knight move can be described in at least two ways.

94. At this point you should practice moving the knight. Diagram 28 shows a sequence of eight knight moves. Study it very carefully and try to trace the same eight moves on your own board, assuming you have one.

95. Knights are the only pieces that can jump over other forces. The only way they can be blocked is if all squares to which they could move are occupied by units of their own forces.

96. In Diagram 29 the white knight can move to any of the squares marked by a star even though there are both friendly and enemy pieces and pawns in the way. Notice that the knight still traces an **L**, as if the blocking units didn't exist.

97. Knights are the only pieces capable of moving in the opening position (all the others are blocked by pawns (see Diagram 2).

98. A knight captures by moving in its normal way and then replacing the opponent's piece or pawn occupying the square to which it transfers.

99. In Diagrams 30 and 31 the knight captures the rook.

100. The knight is the only piece that from move to move must change the color of the square it occupies (Diagram 32). Test this out by moving the knight across the board for a few moves.

Diagram 28
Eight knight moves
Each number in succession
represents the next knight move

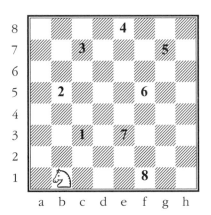

Diagram 29
**The knight can jump over any
piece or pawn**

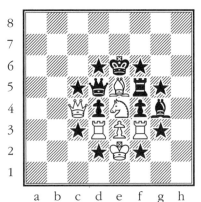

**White's knight can move to any
square marked by a star**

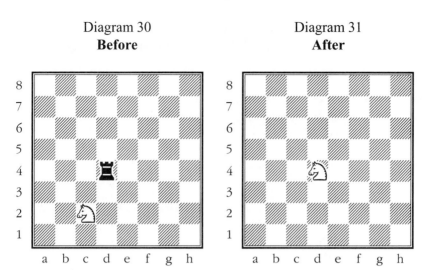

Diagram 30
Before

Diagram 31
After

The knight can capture the rook   The knight has captured the rook

Exercise for the Knight's Move

101. For this exercise all squares are named from the white side. On an empty board place a knight on a1. From a1 maneuver the knight to b1. This takes three moves.

102. One way to do it is to play the knight from a1 to b3, then from b3 to d2, then from d2 to b1. Diagram 33 illustrates this.

Diagram 32
The knight always moves to a square of different color

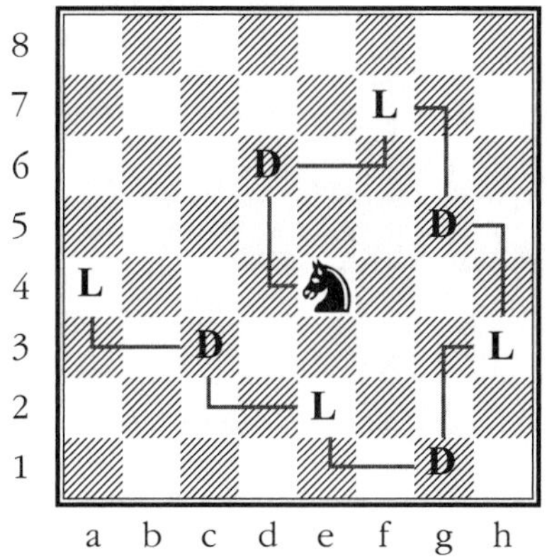

Diagram 33
From a1 to b3 to d2 to b1

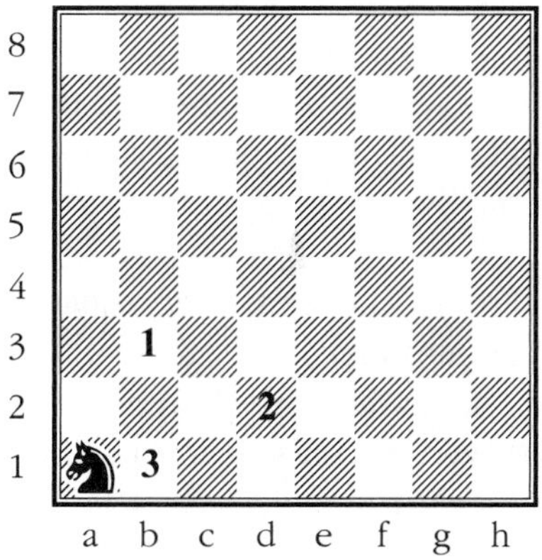

103. Another way to do it is to move the knight from al to c2, then from there to a3, then from there to bl. Mission accomplished. Diagram 34 illustrates this other way.

104. Then, with the same kind of three step maneuver, transfer the knight from bl to cl.

105. This could be done, for example, by moving the knight from bl to c3 to e2 to cl.

106. From cl maneuver the knight to dl, then to el, and so on, until you have maneuvered the knight entirely across White's first rank, stopping at each successive square along the rank every three moves.

Diagram 34
From al to c2 to a3 to bl

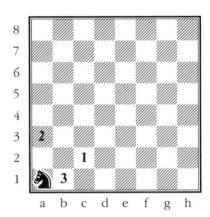

107. From hl then maneuver the knight to h2. Again it takes three moves.

108. One way to do it, for example, is to play the knight from hl to g3 to fl to h2. Diagram 35 illustrates this maneuver.

109. From h2 maneuver the knight across the second rank, in the same way you maneuvered it across the first rank, but this time going left, until the knight reaches the square a2.

110. Then from a2 maneuver the knight to a3. It again takes three moves.

111. From a3, covering every square on the third rank, work the knight across to h3. Use this procedure to maneuver the knight around the entire board, stopping every three

Diagram 35
**Maneuvering the knight
from h1 to h2**

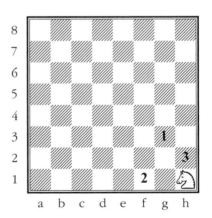

moves on the next square in succession, until each square on the board has been occupied.

112. Try this exercise every day and time it. The faster you complete this version of the knight's tour (there are others, with different requirements), the better your grasp of the knight's movement. In addition this exercise gives practice thinking three moves ahead (actually, three half-moves, since only White's moves are being considered), and thinking ahead is one of the best things a chess player can do.

113. A knight can't:
  (a) capture any of its own forces;
  (b) move to a square occupied by one of its own units;
  (c) capture two or more opposing units on the same turn;
  (d) move without changing the color of the square it occupies.

Review Chart of How the Pieces Move

Piece	How it moves
Rook	along ranks or files from 1-7 squares per move
Bishop	along diagonals from 1-7 squares per move
Queen	along ranks, files, or diagonals from 1-7 squares per move
King	along ranks, files, or diagonals but only one square per move
Knight	like an L in any direction

The Strange World of Pawns

114. I refer to the pawn as being strange because it's truly different from the other kinds of units.

115. Pawns are the foot soldiers – the infantry – of chess. Initially not especially strong, they can often increase in potential as they advance up the board, though not automatically. It depends on how susceptible they become to attack as well as their ability to advance safely and further.

116. Pawns move straight ahead, one square on a turn, vertically up the board for White and vertically down the board for Black.

117. In Diagram 36 the pawn may move to the square marked by the arrow.

118. Pawns can't move backward. They are the only chess units that can't.

119. There's a special rule that applies to each pawn's first move. On the first move you have the option of moving it either one or two squares.

120. Thus, in Diagram 37, the pawn can move to either d3 or d4.

121. Once a pawn has moved, however, it loses the right to move two squares. This is so even if the pawn didn't move two squares on its first move.

Diagram 36
The pawn can move to c4

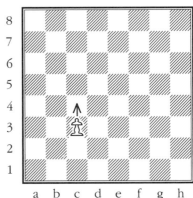

122. Therefore, in Diagram 38, since it would be the pawn's second move, the pawn can move only to e4 and not e5.

123. Every pawn retains the right to move two squares on its first move regardless what other pawns have done.

Diagram 37
**The pawn's initial two
square option**

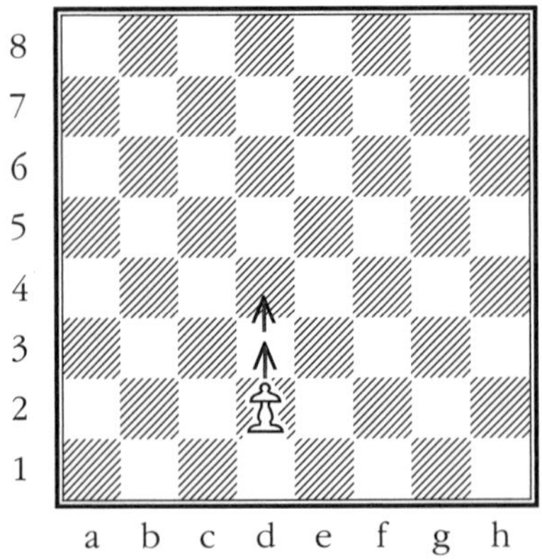

Diagram 38
The pawn can move only to e4

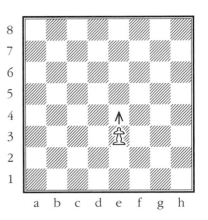

The pawn can move to d3 or d4

124. Pawns are the only units that capture differently from the way they move.

125. Pawns capture one square diagonally ahead.

126. Thus, in Diagrams 39 and 40, the white pawn captures the black rook.

Diagram 39
The pawn may capture the rook or bishop

Diagram 40
The pawn has captured the rook

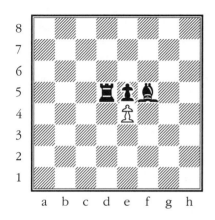
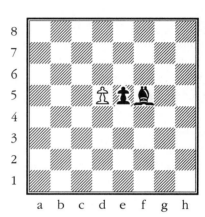

127. Pawns can't capture one square vertically ahead, so in Diagram 39 White's pawn couldn't have captured Black's.

128. Pawns can't capture two squares diagonally ahead. The two-square option does not apply to captures.

Diagram 41
White can't capture Black's pawn

129. Thus, in Diagram 41, White's pawn can't capture Black's, even though White's pawn hasn't moved yet.

130. A pawn can't:
   (a) capture any of its own units;
   (b) move to a square occupied by one of its own units;

(c) capture two or more opposing units on the same turn;

(d) move diagonally;

(e) capture vertically;

(f) move two squares after it's already moved;

(g) move or capture horizontally;

(h) move or capture backward.

131. At the start of a game each side has eight pawns on its second rank. Therefore, the pawns block and prevent the pieces from coming out (except for the knights, which can jump over anything).

132. It turns out that on the first move of a game White has twenty different moves: four knight moves and sixteen pawn moves. Black in turn has a comparable twenty different moves. This means that the first full move of the game can ramify into four hundred different positions. After that, forget about it. No wonder chess is so complex.

133. For the time being this is all you have to know about how the pieces move and the strange world of pawns. Soon you'll encounter a few other rules that apply to these relentless foot soldiers. It'll be for you at that point to judge what it means to be "only a pawn in the game."

Section Four: The Object of the Game

134. Now that you've become acquainted with how the pieces and pawns move you must learn what to do with them.

135. The **object of a chess game** is to capture the enemy king.

136. Paradoxically, you don't actually capture the opposing king, but this will be clarified shortly (see statements 161-162).

137. Here we meet up with two of the most often heard chess terms: "check" and "checkmate." (Checkmate is typically shortened to "mate," and that's how it appears for much of this book.)

138. Before proceeding on to the concepts of check and mate it's useful to familiarize yourself with several other terms.

139. If a unit can capture an opposing unit it's **attacking** it and the action is referred to as an **attack**.

140. But that doesn't mean it's necessarily good to capture the opposing unit or that the attack must be feared.

141. If, however, the attack (that is, the possible capture) leads to advantage or meaningful gain, tangible or intangible, it's also a **threat** and the opposing unit is considered **threatened**.

142. Attacks can be direct or indirect.

143. A **direct attack** implies capture on the next move.

144. An **indirect attack** requires making at least one additional move before producing a direct attack or threat.

145. Attacks don't necessarily have to be answered. In some cases they can even be ignored. But if an attack signifies a real threat it must be dealt with to avoid incurring disadvantage.

146. A direct attack to the king is always a threat. It must be answered by the rules of the game.

147. A direct attack to the king is called **check**.

148. You're **in check** when your king is placed under direct attack by an opposing piece or pawn.

149. You **give check** when one of your own pieces or pawns attacks the opposing king directly.

150. Diagram 42 shows the White king in check from the black bishop.

151. Since losing the king entails losing the game, a player whose king is placed in check must get it **out of check**. The rules require it.

152. There can be as many as three different ways to get out of check:
(a) by blocking the checking attacker (by putting a piece or pawn in the way);
(b) by capturing the checking attacker;
(c) by moving your king to safety.

Diagram 42
The bishop checks White's king

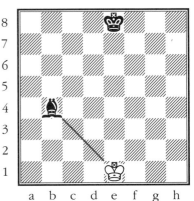

153. Diagrams 43-46 show Black giving check and the three different ways to get out of check.

Diagram 43
The bishop checks

Diagram 44
(a) the knight captures

Diagram 45
(b) the knight blocks

Diagram 46
(c) the king moves

154. If all three ways to get out of check are possible, you may choose any of the three (you may either block, capture, or move to safety).

155. The best option for Diagram 43 is to take the bishop for free, which is choice (a).

156. In other circumstances it might be preferable to reply with either of the other ways to get out of check (moving away or blocking) or even with a different capture of the checking attacker. Naturally, such decisions always depend on specific circumstances.

157. It's illegal:
    (a) to move into check;
    (b) not to get out of check when it's possible;
    (c) to capture a king that illegally moves into check (instead, the illegal king move must be replayed);
    (d) to capture a king that could have, but didn't get out of check (the opponent must take back the illegal move and play a legal one).

158. Suppose your king is suddenly checked and there's no way to prevent its capture on the next move. What then?

159. If you're unable to avoid capture of your king on the next move the game is over: you have been **mated**.

160. In Diagram 47 White is unable to block the bishop's check, capture the bishop, or move the king to a safe square (a square not guarded by any opposing pieces or pawns). White has been checkmated.

161. The game is over as soon as mate is given, when there's no way to avoid the king's capture on the next move. But you don't actually capture the enemy king, as indicated in statement 135.

162. Perhaps not taking the king started as a courtesy in some parts of the world. Then it became a tradition. Now it's a rule and has been so since the Middle Ages. Today it's the way chess is played universally.

Diagram 47
Mate

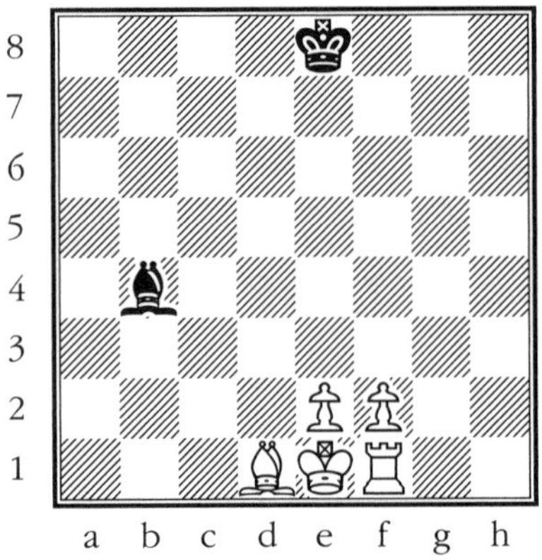

163. To get a feeling for mate, Diagrams 48-51 show you a version of the shortest game possible: Black mates White in two moves.

164. This is called the **Fool's Mate**, which suggests that the result is based less on the winner's skill and more (incredibly more) on the loser's lack of it.

Diagram 48

White's first move:

pawn to f3

Diagram 49

Black's first move:

pawn to e5

Diagram 50

Diagram 51

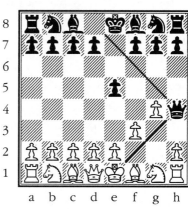

White's second move:
pawn to g4

Black's second move:
queen to h4 mate!

165. It's mate because:
    (a) the white king is in check from the black queen;
    (b) the white king can't escape to a safe square;
    (c) no white piece or pawn can block the check;
    (d) the black queen can't be captured;
    (e) the white king would be captured next move, if the rules allowed it.

166. To reiterate:
    (a) it's just check when the king is directly attacked and its capture **can** be avoided on the next move;
    (b) it's checkmate when the king is directly attacked and its capture **can't** be avoided on the next move.

167. Beginners mistakenly think that check must be announced. Some players even announce check to the queen. There are no such rules.

168. Besides, saying "check" may actually disturb your opponent, causing him or her to lose concentration. Of course, not everyone thinks that's a bad thing to cause.

169. There are three ways to lose a chess game:
    (a) by mate;
    (b) by resignation (giving up);
    (c) by forfeiting on time if you play with a clock.

170. Players generally prefer resigning to being mated. This is true especially for veterans. Maybe it has to do with avoiding embarrassment. Or perhaps it's an acknowledgement of the winner's skill and accomplishment. By resigning it's almost as if the loser is saying, "I see your point," implying a kind of equality with the winner and thereby saving face.

171. But this attitude is not right for newcomers. It's only by being dogged and persistently fighting out hopeless positions in full spirit that introductory players can assimilate winning techniques and methods. Their opponents show and teach them. Over time there's no better way to improve your chess.

172. To put a coda on this, in trying to save yourself you tend to become more resourceful, even salvaging some of those "lost" games. So in order to become a winner you should expect to lose many times. That's part of the schooling process. Besides, **no one ever won a game by resigning**.

Section Five: Mating Patterns

173. In chess, as in many other endeavors, it's necessary to play with a goal in mind.

174. There should be a reason or reasons behind every move.

175. The ultimate goal of chess is to mate the enemy king.

176. Usually, a few friendly chess units working together are needed to give mate.

177. One unit checks the enemy king, while one or more others, sometimes aided by obstructing and poorly placed defending units, keep it from escaping.

178. A successful chess player has a stockpile of mating patterns.

179. A **mating pattern** is a mate given by one or more chess units in a particular way or in a definite formation. There are hundreds of different mating patterns.

180. Diagram 52 shows a mating pattern involving the queen and bishop. Examine the position carefully and make sure that the black king can't avoid being captured on the next move. Remember that the king is never allowed to move into check.

181. It's mate because:
   (a) the bishop checks the black king;
   (b) the bishop can't be blocked or captured;
   (c) the black king has no safe move;
   (d) the black king would be captured on White's next move, if the rules allowed the game to go that far – they don't.

Diagram 52
Black is mated

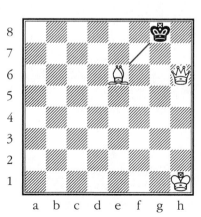

33

182. In Diagram 53 try to find how White can mate Black in one move. Hint: In all problems of this kind, start by looking for moves that check the enemy king.

Diagram 53
White mates in one move

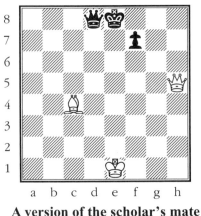

A version of the scholar's mate

Diagram 54
After the queen takes on f7

Black is mated

183. The solution is **Qh5xf7 mate**. (This is read: "Queen on h5 takes on f7 mate.")

184. It's mate because:
(a) the white queen checks the black king;
(b) the white queen can't be captured legally (it's protected by the bishop);
(c) the white queen can't be blocked (there are no intervening squares between it and the black king);
(d) there are no escape squares for the black king;
(e) the black king can't avoid capture on the next move.

Diagram 55
White has taken with the wrong piece

It's not mate and the game continues

185. Note that in Diagram 53 White could instead capture on f7 with the bishop, as in Diagram 55. But that wouldn't be mate: it would only be check and Black's king could move to safety, going to d7, e7, or f8. The game would then continue.

186. In Diagram 56 Black can mate White in one move. Find the move.

Diagram 56
Black mates in one move

Diagram 57
Black has mated White

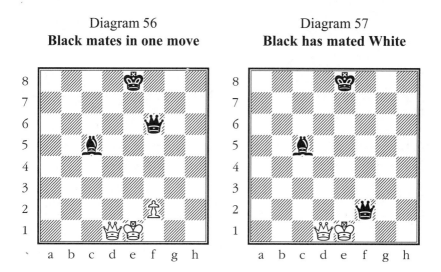

187. Shown in Diagram 57, the solution is **Qf6xf2 mate**. This is read and said: queen on f6 takes on f2 mate. Again, taking with the bishop instead of the queen would give check but not mate.

188. At times different principles may apply. In both Diagrams 53 and 56 checking with the queen is essential to give mate. But what if it weren't mate?

189. In those instances, when you're trying to decide which of two different units should give check on the same square, you must analyze and make a choice based on specifics.

190. Usually checking with the queen is more deadly, but if you're not certain it's also more risky.

191. Furthermore, if it's just check and not mate, you might prefer using the unit of lesser value. Why have the general do what can be done by the private?

192. The same kind of reasoning applies to captures. Sometimes it's better to take with the stronger unit to do more damage. On other occasions it's better to take with the lesser unit to avoid danger or misuse.

193. The only way to decide such conflicts is by the corroboration of concrete analysis.

194. Actually, this suggests one aspect of chess thinking: **the comparison of reasonable alternatives**.

195. For example, let's say you realize your opponent's last move menaces you in some way. You should look for an answer that meets the threat or threats. If it goes well you'll find a move that works.

196. But you shouldn't stop there. After coming up with that possibility you should ask: Do I have another move that's just as good?

197. If you can think of another move or several you've gotten the process going. It enables you to start comparing options, to determine which move satisfies your needs most, and that consideration should lead to your next move.

198. The mates in Diagrams 52-56 show variant outcomes of the same general mating pattern occurring in the opening of some chess games typically appealing to newcomers and children. Illogically, it's known as the **Scholar's Mate**. Yet in "achieving" such victories the winners violate the principles of sound play (we'll go over this a little later). To be sure, win this way too often (like more than once) and your scholarship is apt to come into question.

199. Diagram 58 poses a mate for Black to give in one move. Can you find it?

200. The solution, shown in Diagram 59, is **Rh8-h1 mate**. (This is read: rook on h8 to h1 mate.)

Diagram 58
Black can mate in one move

201. It's mate because:

(a) the rook checks the white king;

(b) the rook can't be captured legally (it's protected by the bishop);

(c) the rook can't be blocked;

(d) the white king has no safe escape square (f1 is guarded by the rook, if the king tries to flee there);

(e) the white king would be captured on the next move.

Diagram 59

White is mated

Section Six: Twenty Mating Patterns

202. Diagrams 60-99 (the next twenty pairs of diagrams) show some common mating patterns. In all cases Black mates White. Cover the answer diagram on the bottom and figure out which unit can be moved in the diagram on the top to mate the white king. Study the diagrams closely: they show how the forces can work together to give mate. Notice that pieces and pawns not directly involved in the mating patterns might not be shown. This means it may not be necessary to include the black king, though in each diagram it's there for formality.

Diagram 60
Black mates in one move

Diagram 61
White is mated

Solution: the rook mates

Diagram 62
Black mates in one move

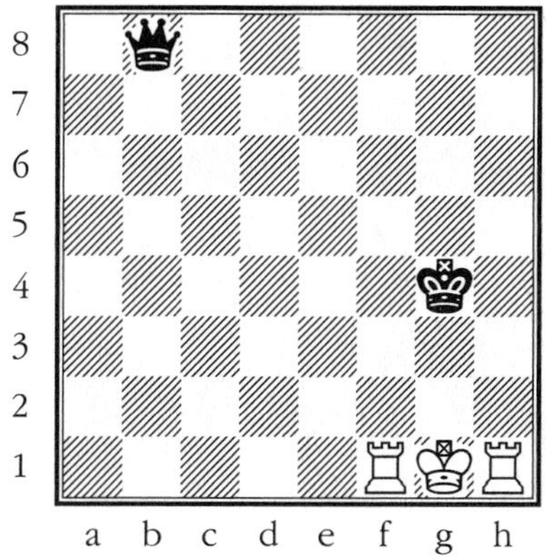

Diagram 64
Black mates in one move

Diagram 63
White is mated

Solution: the queen mates

Diagram 65
White is mated

Solution: the knight mates

Diagram 66
Black mates in one move

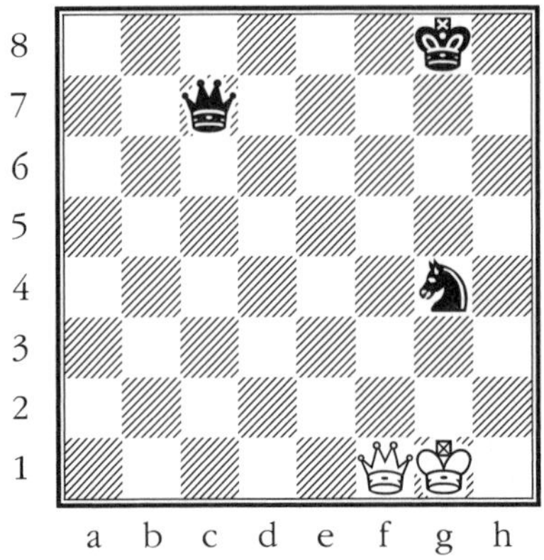

Diagram 68
Black mates in one move

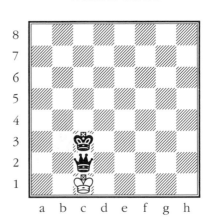

Diagram 67
White is mated

Solution: the queen mates

Diagram 69
White is mated

Solution: the queen mates

Diagram 70
Black mates in one move

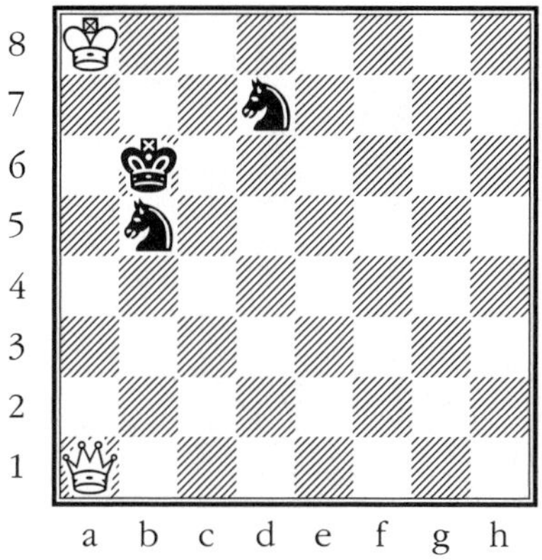

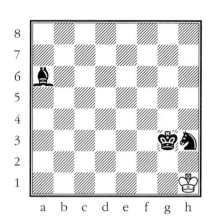

Diagram 72
Black mates in one move

Diagram 71
White is mated

Solution: the knight on c7 mates

Diagram 73
White is mated

Solution: the bishop mates

41

Diagram 74
Black mates in one move

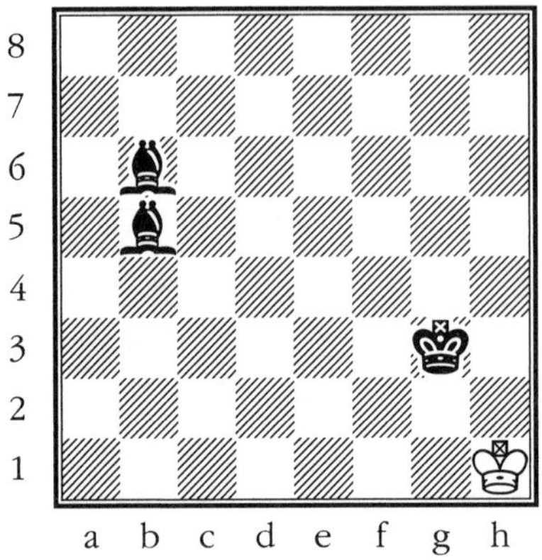

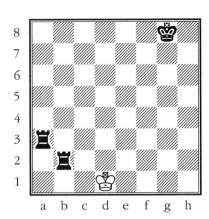

Diagram 76
Black mates in one move

Diagram 75
White is mated

Solution: the bishop on c6 mates

Diagram 77
White is mated

Solution: the rook on a1 mates

Diagram 78
Black mates in one move

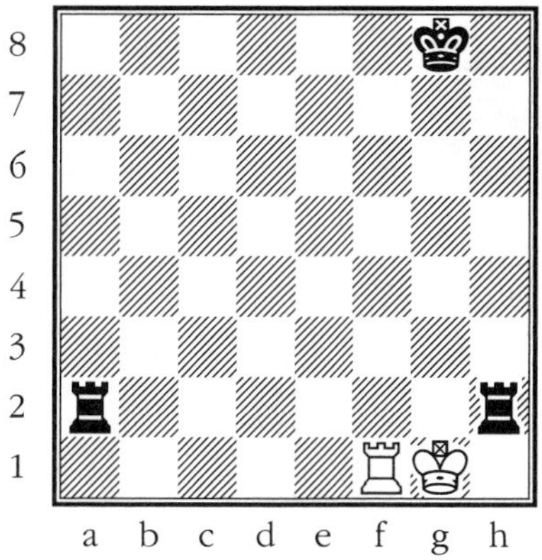

Diagram 80
Black mates in one move

Diagram 79
White is mated

Solution: the rook on g2 mates

Diagram 81
White is mated

Solution: the queen mates

Diagram 82
Black mates in one move

Diagram 84
Black mates in one move

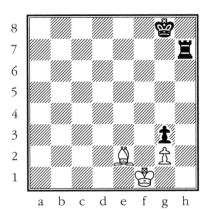

Diagram 83
White is mated

Solution: the queen mates

Diagram 85
White is mated

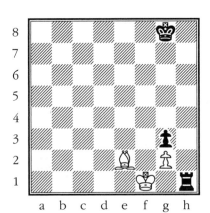

Solution: the rook mates

Diagram 86
Black mates in one move

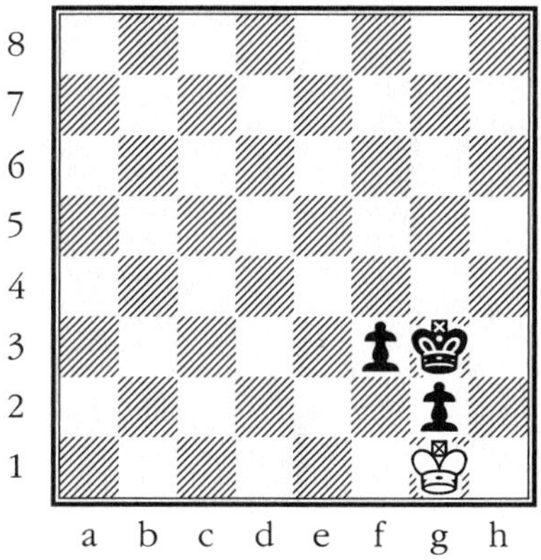

Diagram 88
Black mates in one move

Diagram 87
White is mated

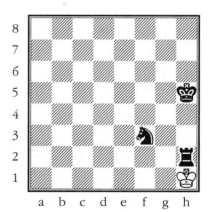

Solution: the pawn mates

Diagram 89
White is mated

Solution: the rook mates

Diagram 90
Black mates in one move

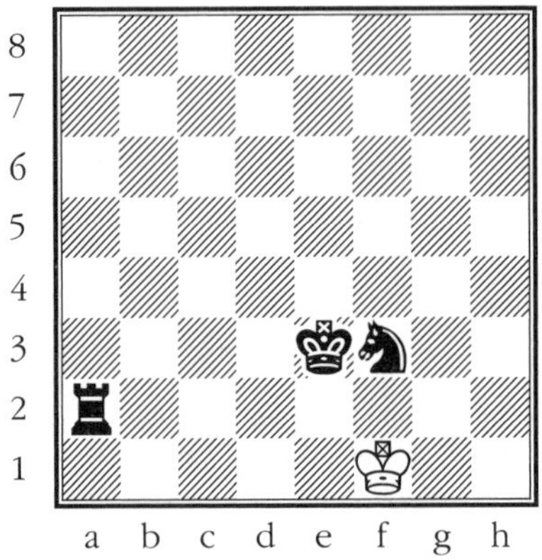

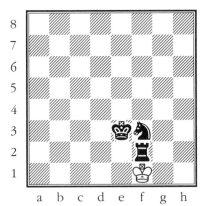

Diagram 92
Black mates in one move

Diagram 91
White is mated

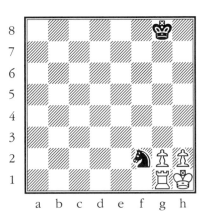

Solution: the rook mates

Diagram 93
White is mated

Solution: the knight mates

Diagram 94
Black mates in one move

Diagram 96
Black mates in one move

Diagram 95
White is mated

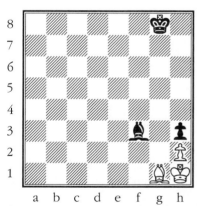

Solution: the bishop mates

Diagram 97
White is mated

Solution: the knight mates

Diagram 98
Black mates in one move

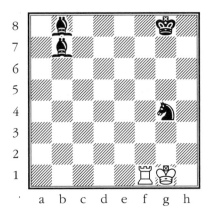

Diagram 99
White is mated

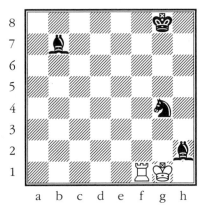

Solution: the bishop mates

203. Mating problems to be solved in one move are seldom difficult, but mating problems to be solved in two or more moves often are.

204. There are further distinctions. Some mates arise naturally in real games. They may contain units unnecessary and irrelevant to the mating pattern. These problems or tactics can be hard or easy depending on circumstances (what can happen in the game).

205. Other mates are **composed problems**. If they're done right and adhere to aesthetic principles there should be no unneeded material present. These mates can be very difficult.

206. Mating problems are described in specific ways. "White to play and mate in two moves" means that White plays a move, Black responds, and then White gives mate. White plays two moves and Black plays one move.

207. "Black to play and mate in two moves" therefore means that Black plays a move, White responds, and then Black gives mate. In other words, Black plays two moves and White plays just one.

208. In strict chess jargon **a full move** consists of a move both sides. In accordance with this terminology – which is also the language of computer programming – a move for just one player is considered **a half move**.

209. In effect "Black to play and mate in two moves" means that Black plays two half moves and White plays only one. But most discussions between average players seldom resort to half-move distinctions, so that kind of move-splitting won't be employed here either.

210. Some problems in chess books require that you look further ahead than two moves. Trying to look ahead raises a problem: how can you see your opponent's responses? You know where you're planning to move, or at least you think you do, but how can you determine how your opponent's going to reply?

211. Chess problems can be difficult for various reasons. One aspect of a chess problem's difficulty depends on the number of plausible responses the defender may have. The more the number of reasonable opposing replies, the more complex the problem is likely to be.

212. If a particular response is the only legal or practical move it's said to be **forced**.

213. The easiest problems to solve are those that force the opponent to respond with a particular move or with any of just a few moves. If a response is compulsory, or essentially forced, it's then easier to see ahead to what the opponent must do or is likely to do.

214. Generally, the most forcing moves are threats to checkmate or win significant material. These threats should be answered to avoid immediate or eventual loss.

215. Since every check is a forcing move, it's typically prudent to begin a real-game mating puzzle by considering any logical check you may have.

216. Besides limiting your opponent's options a check also renders your analysis more manageable. It's by searching for forcing moves such as checks, especially in series, that players can look further ahead, trying to see and control more distant outcomes.

217. So if you want to analyze in your mind: **look for forcing moves**.

218. A check is indeed a forcing move, but this doesn't mean that checks are automatically good and should be played without further thought.

219. A bad check can lead to an opposing response that gives the defender an advantage. There are various ways this could happen.

220. For example, if your opponent threatens you and you ignore the threat, instead giving an ill-considered check, your opponent may be able to answer your check with a new threat.

221. Suddenly you must cope with the new threat as well as the old one ignored on the previous move. It might not be possible to reply adequately to both.

222. The next problem allows the defender only one possible response to the correct first move (hint: look for a check). It's not as hard as you might first think.

223. Diagram 100 illustrates a position where White can play and mate Black in two moves.

224. Try to solve the problem in your mind, without setting it up on a real chessboard for analytic practice, but don't be alarmed if you have difficulty. The ability to look ahead comes with experience.

Diagram 100
**White to play and
mate in two moves**

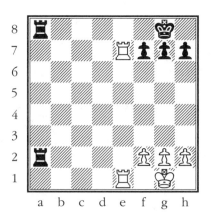

225. If you've looked ahead carefully and properly you've undoubtedly determined that White's correct first move is Re7-e8+. This is read "rook on e7 moves to e8 check." Black must then answer the check by capturing White's rook, Ra8xe8, which is read "rook on a8 takes on e8," where the "x" signifies a capture. Finally, White's best second move is to take back, Re1xe8 mate. This is read "rook on e1 takes on e8 mate." The final position, seen at first in your mind, and now on the page, is displayed in Diagram 101.

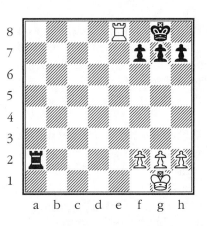

Diagram 101
Black has been mated

226. Review this section carefully. If you have trouble with it, go on. For now it's enough that you have been introduced to mating patterns and some ways to think about them. You can worry about mastering these ideas subsequently. An old Chinese proverb says that a journey of a thousand miles begins with a single step. In step to the beat of that steady drum, let's proceed to our next destination.

Section Seven: Three Special Rules

Castling

227. Because the king is so vulnerable chess has a special rule to help protect it, which supersedes the rule of moving only one piece on a turn.

228. This special rule is called **castling** and it's the only time during a game that two pieces can be moved on the same turn.

229. In Diagram 101 the squares on the first rank between the king and rook are unoccupied. If both the king and rook have not yet moved in the game then White may castle.

230. Castling is done by moving the king two squares toward the rook (in this case to g1) and then moving the rook to the other side of the king (in this case to f1). Diagram 102 shows what the position looks like after castling kingside.

231. There are two kinds of castling:
>(a) **castling kingside**, also known as castling short; and
>(b) **castling queenside**, also known as castling long.

232. In Diagram 103 you're to assume that neither king or rook have previously moved. Black castles queenside by moving the king two squares toward the rook, in this case to c8, and then moving the rook to the other side of the king, in this case to d8 (Diagram 104).

Diagram 101
Before castling

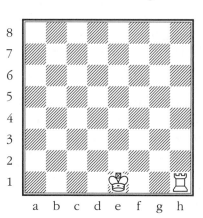

Diagram 102
After castling

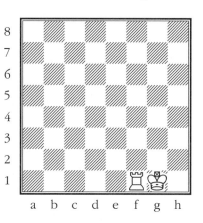

52

Diagram 103
Before castling queenside

Diagram 104
After castling queenside

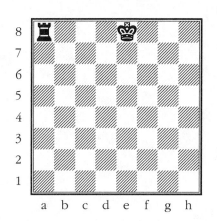

233. Both White and Black are allowed to castle just once during a game.

234. Usually both sides exercise their castling rights, which are also described as castling privileges.

235. Kingside castling happens more frequently than queenside castling, mainly because it's easier, since there's one less piece to clear out – the queen.

236. There are three additional factors that would make castling impossible:
   (a) if the castling king is already in check;
   (b) if the castling king would wind up in check;
   (c) if the castling king must pass through check (over a square guarded by the opponent).

237. In Diagram 105 castling is impossible because the white king is **in check**.

238. If the checking bishop could be blocked, captured, or driven away, then White could castle on the next move or any move after that, assuming the move remains legal.

239. Diagrams 105-108 show White being in check, then blocking the check, Black then moving the bishop to safety, and then White castling after that.

Diagram 105
White is in check and can't castle

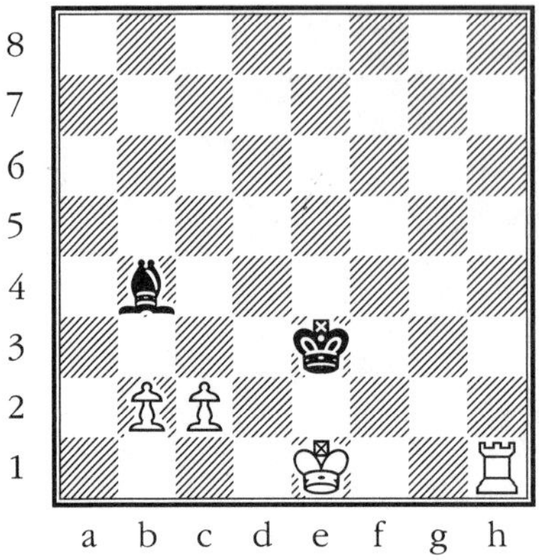

Diagram 106
White blocks the check

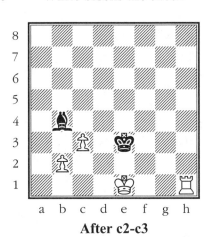

After c2-c3

Diagram 107
The bishop moves to safety

After Bb4-a5

Diagram 108
**No longer checked,
White is able to castle**

After castling

240. In Diagram 109, since g8 is guarded by the bishop, castling is not legal because Black's king would be castling **into check**.

241. But the bishop could be captured by the knight (Diagram 110). After White takes back (Diagram 111), Black could then castle kingside (Diagram 112).

Diagram 109
Black can't castle into check

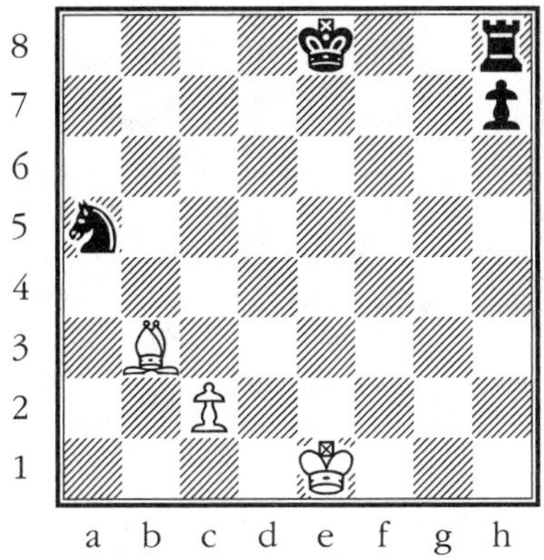

Diagram 110
So Black first captures the bishop

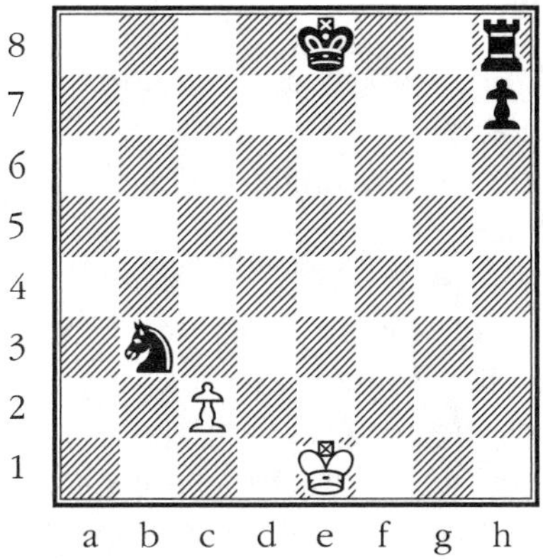

After Na5xb3

Diagram 111
After White takes back

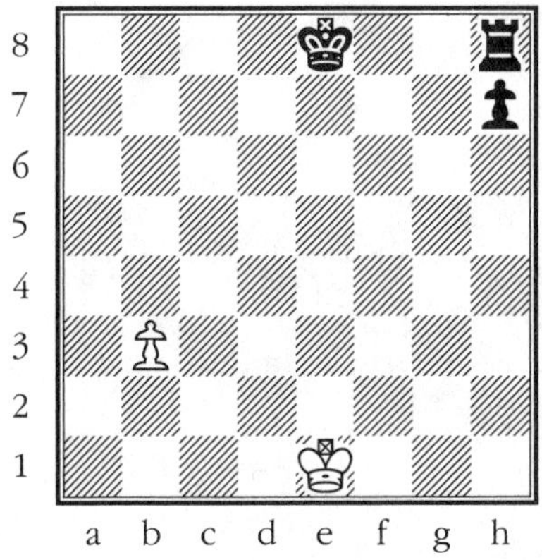

After c2xb3

Diagram 112
Then Black can castle

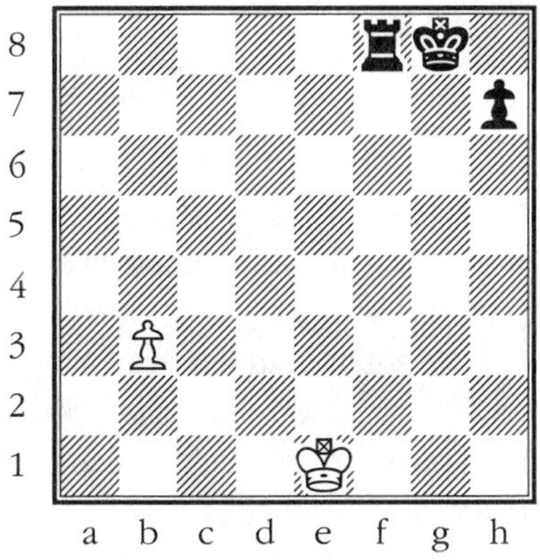

After castling kingside

55

242. In order to castle kingside in Diagram 113 the white king would have to pass **through check** (over a square guarded by the black rook on f7).

243. Even though in Diagram 113 the king doesn't stop on f1, the rules prevent White from castling kingside. If somehow the black rook at f7 could be blocked, driven away, or captured, then afterward White still could castle kingside.

Diagram 113
White can't castle kingside

Since f1 is guarded

244. But White doesn't have to wait until then to castle, since castling queenside is available, which is illustrated in Diagram 114.

245. Note that in Diagram 113 it's okay for White's a1-rook to pass over a square guarded by Black (the square b1) as long as White's king doesn't pass through check or wind up in check, and it doesn't.

Diagram 114
But White can castle queenside

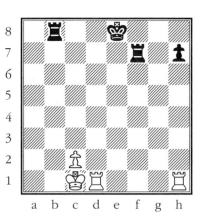

246. Castling may happen at any time during the game, assuming it's a legal move.

247. To summarize, you can't castle if:

    (a) king or castling rook has already moved, even if you then move the relevant piece back to where it started;
    (b) the squares in between king and castling rook are blocked;
    (c) you've already castled earlier;
    (d) you're in check;
    (e) you would have to move into check;
    (f) you would have to move through check.

Section Eight: Drawing a Chess Game

248. It's possible for a chess game to end without anyone winning or losing. Games that end in this way are called draws.

249. There are five different ways to draw a chess game:
- (a) stalemate;
- (b) the fifty-move rule;
- (c) insufficient mating material;
- (d) threefold repetition;
- (e) agreement.

Stalemate

250. If the side whose turn it is to play has no legal move, and is not in check, then the game is drawn by **stalemate**.

251. If one side has been stalemated the other has given the stalemate.

252. Diagrams 115-118 illustrate the concept of stalemate. In each case it's Black's turn, Black is not in check, but there's no legal move, so the game is drawn.

Diagram 115
Black is stalemated

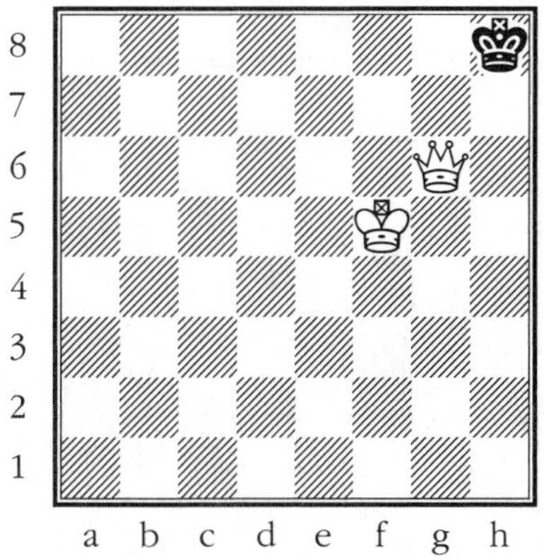

Diagram 116
Black is stalemated

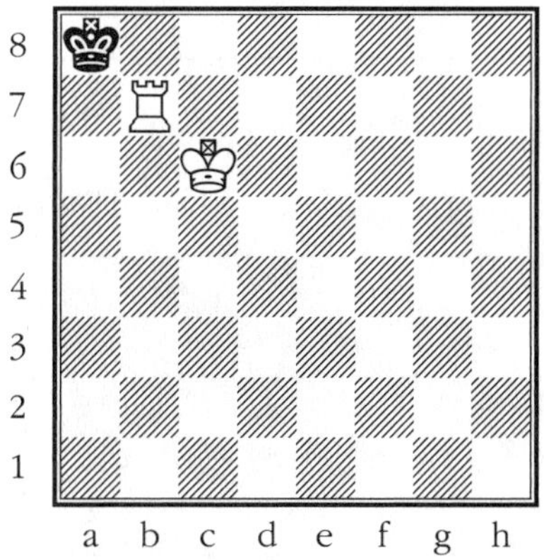

57

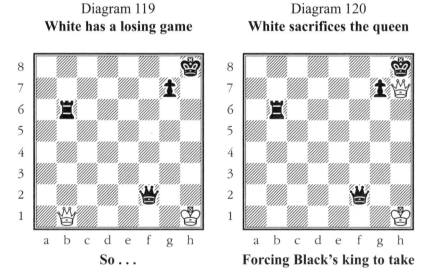

Diagram 117
Black is stalemated

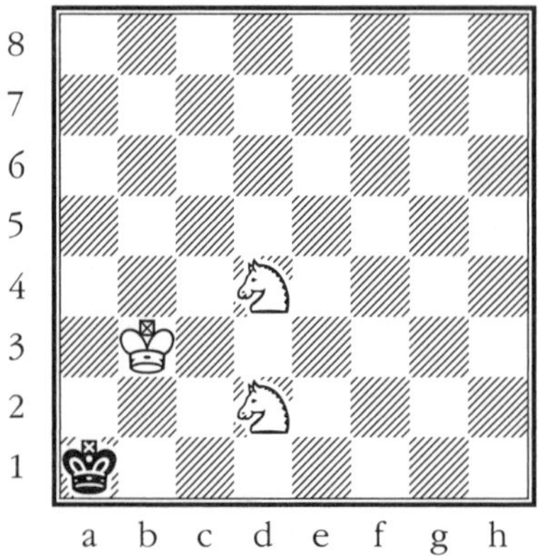

Diagram 118
Black is stalemated

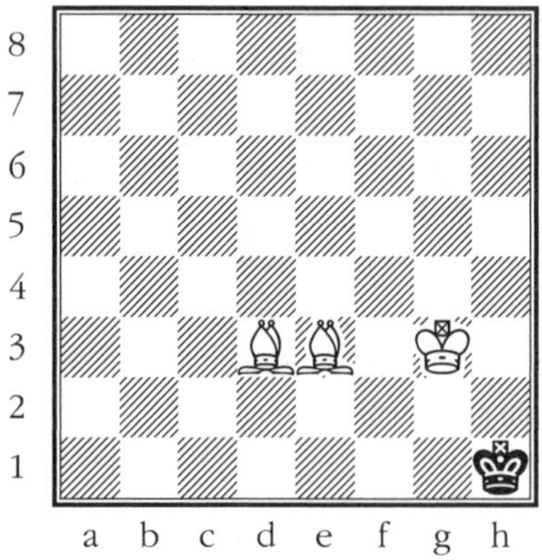

253. This possibility of drawing a game when hopelessly behind in material is why most beginners stick it out to the very last man. Not surprisingly, some very famous chess games have ended in this way, with the side on the verge of losing sacrificing their remaining forces to produce a situation with no legal moves, yet with the king not being in check.

254. Diagram 119 offers a slightly more complicated instance, where the stalemate has to be set up. White to play has a losing game.

Diagram 119
White has a losing game

So . . .

Diagram 120
White sacrifices the queen

Forcing Black's king to take

255. Rather than go down to defeat White can sacrifice the queen by moving to h7 (Diagram 120). Black has no choice but to capture White's queen. After doing so (Diagram 121) White doesn't have a legal move and isn't in check. The game is drawn by stalemate – a case of less being more.

The Fifty-Move Rule

256. If fifty moves have been played, without either a piece being captured or a pawn being moved, then the player whose turn it is may claim a draw.

Diagram 121
White is stalemated

257. If the above two conditions are fulfilled a draw can be claimed regardless of all other circumstances.

258. There are exceptions. You can't claim a draw if you've been mated (though illegal moves must be played for mate to be a repetition.)

259. You also can't claim a draw if you've already played your move and it's your opponent's turn. You'd have to wait for the next opportunity, hoping that one arises.

260. Some players mistakenly think that the fifty-move rule is really a fifteen-move rule, a sixteen-move rule, or a twenty-one move rule. It isn't, it isn't, and it isn't. There are no such shortcuts to drawing heaven.

261. The fifty-move rule is seldom used because it's easy to get around. For example, let's say forty moves have been played and counted. In ten more moves the side that desires a draw can claim one. Yet if anyone moves a pawn or captures a piece or pawn the count must start all over again. Even as late as move forty-nine of the inclusive sequence you still could be forced to start the count all over if either a pawn is moved or a capture is made.

262. If you're playing a tournament game, and you claim a draw by the fifty-move rule, you must be able to prove that the appropriate number of moves were played. It helps if you have an accurate score sheet. Otherwise, you better be persuasive enough to convince the tournament director of your claim's correctness. Good luck.

Insufficient Mating Material

263. A draw also results if neither side has enough material left to force mate.

264. For example, a lone king can't mate a lone king, since neither side can move into check.

265. While a king can protect a unit that gives mate (such a finale being referred to as a **support mate**), it can't give mate itself since it's against the rules for a king to move into check.

266. Beginners often are mislead by the popular expression "a king can't take a king."

267. This colloquialism is supposed to indicate that a king is given *carte blanche* to move right next to the opposing king. But the existence of this saying doesn't mean that your king is free to violate the rules. Charming thought or not, you can't move into check with impunity, and no player – or king – has license to transgress the rules.

268. Two other examples of drawing by insufficient mating material:
    (a) one side has only a king and bishop, and the other only a king;
    (b) one side has only a king and knight, and the other only a king.

269. Test these situations out on a chessboard. For both of them you won't even be able to set up a mate, let alone force mate through playing.

Threefold Repetition

270. If the exact position occurs three or more times during a chess game, the player whose turn it is may claim a draw by the threefold repetition rule.

271. The repetitions need not occur on consecutive moves. They may happen at any points during the game.

272. A position is not really repeated unless every single detail is the same. Every unit must be on the same square. Every unit must have the same potential. And the same player must also be on the move.

273. Don't think that a draw can be claimed if merely the same move is repeated three times. That's another common misconception.

274. What's not a misconception is that in tournament play you may have to substantiate your claim with an accurate score sheet.

275. If all requirements are fulfilled, the draw may be claimed by the player who is about to repeat the position for the third time, just before he or she executes the third repetition.

276. It must be your turn in order to claim a draw by a threefold repetition. Don't make your move and then claim it.

277. Once you've moved it's already your opponent's turn and it's too late to claim a draw.

278. If your opponent offers the opportunity for another chance at the same repetition, however, and you can still prove your claim that the position is about to be repeated at least for the third time, you can call over the tournament director and establish your claim. If it's not a tournament, you're on your own.

Agreement

279. The most common way to draw a game is for one side to propose a draw and for the other to accept. Something like ninety-five percent of real draws arise in this way.

280. The correct way to offer a draw (as opposed to claiming a draw by the threefold repetition rule) is to make your move and then propose the draw. That way your opponent can think about it.

281. After your opponent has thought about it he or she will accept your offer or decline it.

282. If your opponent plays a move without orally responding the offer is considered to be declined and the game goes on.

283. Obviously most of us would prefer to win rather than draw. But if your situation is looking fairly hopeless, finding a way to draw allows you to salvage something from the game.

284. Chess is a **zero sum game**, which means the winner's gain is equal the loser's loss.

285. This is reflected in tournament play by individual chess games being awarded one point to be divided up between the combatants.

286. The winner gets one point; the loser gets nothing; and if the players draw they get half a point each. The total points in the result always adds up to one.

287. You may not want to draw, but if you're headed toward defeat, half a point is surely better than nothing. Major tournaments and matches are frequently decided by a timely rescue of a crucial half point.

Section Nine: Pawn Promotion

288. Pawns are the only chess units that can change into other units: they can become any of the pieces except the king.

289. Since pawns can't move backward it would seem that once a pawn reaches its eighth rank it has nowhere to go. The rule of **pawn promotion**, however, changes the whole picture.

290. When a pawn reaches its last rank it must be promoted. This means it must be changed into a piece (either a knight, bishop, rook, or queen).

291. Diagrams 122 and 123 show a promotion sequence (before and after). In Diagram 122 the pawn starts on f7. Diagram 123 shows the pawn having been converted to a queen on f8.

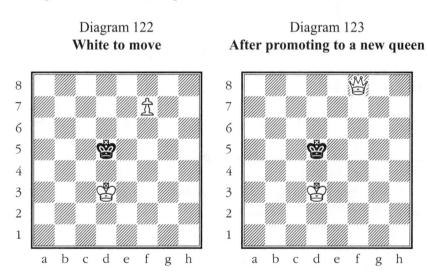

Diagram 122　　　　　　　　Diagram 123
White to move　　**After promoting to a new queen**

292. Since most players are likely to promote to a queen, the most powerful piece, pawn promotion is commonly referred to as **queening a pawn**.

293. Promoting to any piece other than a queen is known as **underpromotion**.

294. Why would you underpromote? Why might you want a unit less valuable than a queen?

295. One reason would be to avoid stalemate. By making a rook instead of a queen you might prevent stalemate and still mate shortly thereafter.

296. Or you may want to execute an immediate tactic. By making a knight instead of a queen you might give mate or win the enemy queen with a forking check.

297. But these are special circumstances, and most of the time one simply makes a new queen and that's that.

298. To be sure, this possibility of a pawn's transformation into a queen is often the winning factor in a chess game. An extra queen almost always wins.

299. Each pawn upon reaching its eighth rank may be promoted, regardless of how many pawns have already been promoted for either side.

300. Consequently, it's theoretically possible for a player to make as many as eight new pieces, of any kind or in any ratio.

301. One exception is that you can't make a new king.

302. Another exception is that both players can't make eight new pieces. That would add up to a total of sixteen new pieces, and the arithmetic of the board doesn't allow that. (Try it and see.)

303. But for a single player, if all eight pawns remarkably sneak through, it's permissible (though almost always terribly imprudent, and probably improbable) to make as many as eight new queens.

304. Or, if you prefer, you can make as many knights, bishops, rooks, or queens as you'd like, in any combination, as long as the total doesn't exceed eight new pieces (it can't).

305. A common misconception is that it's illegal to have two or more bishops of the same color (bishops that travel on squares of the same color). There is no such restriction.

306. Another misconception is that you can only promote to a piece that has already come off the board by a previous exchange. This isn't a rule either.

307. A piece made through promotion has the same powers as a natural one. A promoted knight is identical to a natural knight, a promoted bishop is identical to a natural bishop, and so on.

308. As soon as a pawn is moved to its eighth rank it must be promoted. If an extra queen is not available – or any other piece of your choosing – state what piece you want the pawn to become and distinguish it in some way, if you can.

309. For example, some players tie rubber bands around newly promoted pawns to avoid confusion with pawns that haven't been promoted. Or, if Scotch tape is available, some players put tape on the pawn.

310. But most of the civilized world prefers using an upside down rook. If the rook isn't flat enough at the top, that's another problem. You're a chess player: you solve it.

311. Whatever piece you turn a pawn into, it must stay as that piece for the remainder of the game. Once a pawn is promoted to a knight it's always a knight.

312. Promoted pieces are just as vulnerable to capture as natural ones. Promoted pieces have no additional or special powers.

313. As a point of advice don't promote too many pawns to new queens, since you increase the chance for giving stalemate. A superiority of one queen is, barring very unusual circumstances, almost always enough advantage to force eventual mate.

314. To summarize, a pawn can't:
   (a) promote to a king;
   (b) remain as a pawn after promotion;
   (c) change to a different kind of unit after it has been promoted to a particular one.

Section Ten: En Passant

315. If you have trouble with this section you may be able to skip it for now. It's not immediately relevant to what follows and can be reconsidered later. But don't forget about it because the possibility of its occurrence is integral to the game.

316. The least understood and most questioned rule of chess is the rule of *en passant*. (Many people play chess without even knowing this rule.) It refers to a certain kind of pawn capture.

317. *En passant* is a French expression that means in passing. If a pawn tries to pass an opposing pawn by moving two squares, it can be captured in passing.

318. You can capture en passant or be captured *en passant*.

319. We see how this works in the next three diagrams. In Diagram 124 it's Black's move.

320. Suppose Black moves the d-pawn two squares ahead, from d7 to d5 (let's say, trying to avoid being captured). This gives us Diagram 125.

Diagram 124
Black to move

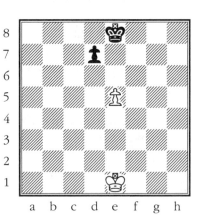

321. White in essence may pretend Black's pawn had moved only one square, capturing it as if it had advanced only one square. Diagram 126 shows the position after White captures Black's pawn *en passant*.

322. Restating this slightly:
(a) if you have a pawn on your fifth rank;
(b) and your opponent has an unmoved pawn on an adjacent file;

Diagram 125
After Black's move

Diagram 126
After White captures on d6
en passant

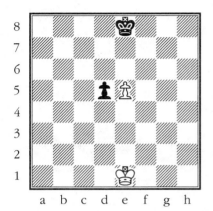

(c) and your opponent advances the pawn two squares;

(d) you may pretend the pawn advanced only one square;

(e) and your pawn may capture the opposing pawn as if it had advanced only one square.

323. Diagrams 127-129 show Black capturing *en passant*.

Diagram 127
White to move

Diagram 128
After White has moved the pawn
two squares

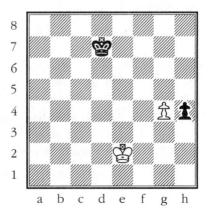

324. In determining the possibility of an *en passant* capture you must consider the fifth rank from your point of view. It has nothing to do with algebraic notation. So don't be confused by the number "5" at the side of a diagram or sometimes appearing on the perimeter of an actual chessboard.

325. The pawn able to make the capture must be capable of being passed by a two-square advance.

Diagram 129
Black has captured *en passant*

326. Thus we see a possible reason for the rule's logic and creation: to prevent a player from suddenly locking up the game. *En passant* captures make it possible to keep the lines open and clear.

327. You don't have to capture a pawn *en passant* simply because you can. You may ignore the possibility of capture and play another move instead.

328. But if you want to capture *en passant* you must do it on your very next move.

329. If you delay the capture of an enemy pawn *en passant* for even one move, you lose the right to capture that particular pawn in the *en passant* way.

330. For further clarification take a look at Diagram 130. It shows a situation where the black side has a pawn on its fifth rank and White's adjacent pawn has already moved one square previously.

Diagram 130
White to move

331. If White's pawn now advances to d4 (Diagram 131), can Black capture it *en passant*?

332. No, Black can't capture the white pawn *en passant* since it hadn't moved two squares in one move. White's pawn had previously moved.

333. During the course of a game (and if the situation arises):
(a) any pawn may capture or be captured *en passant*;
(b) both White and Black may capture *en passant* as many times as possible and desired.

Diagram 131
After advancing to d4

Black can't capture *en passant*

334. Just because an *en passant* capture is possible doesn't mean it's desirable. So don't necessarily avoid making a two-square pawn advance because your opponent can capture *en passant*. You may be able to take back without loss and the overall affect may be neutral or to your advantage.

335. By a similar token don't forget about the rule either, advancing a pawn two squares ahead, thinking perhaps you're avoiding capture, when suddenly your opponent takes your pawn *en passant*. Such a transaction could be unsettling, if it doesn't result in you obtaining a lost game.

336. For instance, in Diagram 132, White to play would be in serious trouble if the b-pawn advances two squares, trying to head toward making a new queen at b8. The shocker would be that Black could take White's pawn *en passant* (Diagrams 133-134). Soon Black would be the one doing the queening.

Diagram 132
White shouldn't advance the b-pawn

69

Diagram 133
White has advanced
two squares

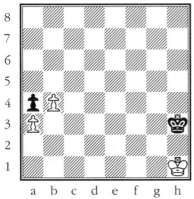

And now Black can

capture *en passant*

Diagram 134
Black soon makes a
new queen at b1

White has blundered

away the game

Section Eleven: The Exchange Values of the Pieces

337. The object of chess is to checkmate the opposing king, but as we've already said, this isn't always so easy.

338. Usually before you can force checkmate you must have some concrete, clear advantage.

339. What it's really about is gaining control. You can gain control if you have the advantage.

340. Many different factors determine who has the ultimate advantage in a chess position. The easiest factor to weigh is the strength of the armies. If you have the stronger army, or your material can do more, usually you should be able to force checkmate given enough time.

341. Advantages in material are not only determined by the number of units but also by the kind. Generally, a unit's relative value is based on the number of squares it can move to, guard, and influence.

342. But circumstances also play a role. In many situations better deployed forces can outgun underutilized material superiority.

343. Piece values are always capable of being temporarily affected by circumstances.

344. Mobility, for instance, can raise or lower the immediate worth of any piece.

345. The term mobility generally refers to the number of different squares a piece can move to in any given position. The more squares a piece can move to the greater its **mobility**.

346. Nevertheless, sometimes you can have decent mobility but your opponent controls all or many of the desirable squares you'd like to use. Perhaps he or she dominates more territory.

347. Some of this is based on how far advanced your center pawns are. Generally, the further advanced your central pawn front, the greater the element of space you command.

348. Space and mobility are related terms. If a piece has greater mobility than another it tends to observe more space than another.

349. Much of chess has to do with exchanging forces, bartering this for that. Since the possibility of exchanging fuels so much of the game's activity, it's imperative that you be able to evaluate each transaction.

350. In capturing try to get at least as much as you give up.

351. Before examining the relative values of the forces remember that:
(a) you win material when you get more than you give up;
(b) you lose material when you get less than you give up;
(c) you trade material when you get the same as you give up (or if you get an amount of material adding up to an equal total value).

352. Introductory players occasionally say "lose" when they really mean "trade." You're not losing any material if you get the same unit in return, say a knight for a knight or a rook for a rook.

353. Nor are you losing material if you obtain a comparable amount in value, though these equivalent situations must be judged a little more carefully.

354. Disastrous as it may be, it's not uncommon for players to ruin their positions just to avoid trading queens.

355. One contention by newcomers is that they especially like or need their queen. Perhaps their opponents don't particularly like or need their queens as much. Naturally, such logic is absurd.

356. So get used to the idea that exchanging is an indispensable part of the game. You can't horde your forces hoping to capture your opponent's pieces and pawns for nothing. Actually you can, but with such a strategy don't expect to win many chess games.

357. Since pawns are the most basic units they serve as the currency of exchange. That is, the value of everything else is expressed in pawns.

358. Naturally, a pawn is worth one pawn. So assuming other factors weigh reasonably for you, you should be willing to exchange a pawn for a pawn.

359. But a pawn's placement is not irrelevant. There can be dangerously advanced pawns or weakened pawns subject to attack.

360. You wouldn't necessarily want to trade a sick pawn for a healthy one. So the quality of the unit is a factor. But all things being essentially equal, trading a pawn for a pawn is fine.

361. The next valuable unit is the knight. It's worth about three pawns. So you should be willing to exchange a knight for another knight, or even for three pawns, if the situation seems to be conducive.

362. Bishops are about equal to knights, though both pieces obviously have different powers. Accordingly, these two kinds of pieces should be slightly different in value.

363. Yet it's practical to consider them roughly comparable, worth about three pawns each.

364. Thus, if things seem to be otherwise working out, you should be willing to exchange a bishop for another bishop, for a knight, or for three pawns.

365. Bishops and knights are known as **minor pieces**, each having a general value of about three pawns.

366. Queens and rooks are **major pieces**.

367. In common chess parlance, when you say you're ahead by a piece, you mean that you're ahead by either a bishop or knight.

368. A rook is worth about five pawns. So in addition to exchanging it for another rook, under the right conditions it would also be okay to trade it for a bishop and two pawns, a knight and two pawns, or five pawns.

369. A queen is worth slightly more than the combination of its component powers (rook and bishop).

370. A queen is worth about nine pawns, whereas a rook and bishop together would be worth about eight pawns. What accounts for this disparity?

371. The difference is somewhat reflected in the concept of synergy, where the whole tends to be greater than the sum of its parts.

372. In most reasonable instances, if key factors also support the operation, you should be willing to trade a queen for another queen or for some other combination of forces adding up to about nine pawns in value.

373. On some occasions you might even consider getting slightly less material in return for a queen if other determinants line up on your side of the ledger.

374. Still, you should never just "exchange" equivalent values in combinations of different units.

375. Before doing that you should look ahead and see which grouping of force is likely to be favored by the resulting position. That's a judgment call, and it's not so easy to make when mulling over material medleys.

376. The king doesn't have an exchange value. Why? Because it can never be exchanged: the rules of the game don't permit it.

377. Nevertheless, a king does influence all the squares in its immediate surrounding area. So in terms of attack and defense a king is generally worth about four pawns.

378. This means in many positions, if we consider just capability, that a king is stronger than either a bishop or knight.

379. That's why a principle of the endgame, the final phase of a chess game, recommends getting the king back into action as soon as reasonably possible.

380. Thus the maxim: **The king is a strong piece. Use it.**

381. Don't forget these values are relative. They can temporarily go up or down based on circumstances.

382. Regardless how valuable a unit is, you should be willing to sacrifice it to force an immediate checkmate or to obtain a winning position.

383. To restate what by now should be obvious, various factors, direct or indirect, tangible or intangible, strategic or tactical, could impact a piece's relative value.

384. For example, if a piece is placed badly, it's value tends to be reduced. If a piece is placed well, it's value tends to be increased.

385. An aggressive bishop may be more precious than a passively hampered rook, while a centralized knight may be even more deadly than a queen, especially if poised and tactics are favorable.

386. The key point is that the standard values of the forces are not absolute: time, circumstance, and other relations influence them. In the overwhelming majority of positions, however, these values can be trusted and used to help render evaluations.

Section Twelve: How to Record a Game

387. It's possible to keep a written record of the moves of a chess game. Writing the moves down is called **keeping score**. You can read a chess game as you can a musical composition.

388. In keeping score moves are not written out but abbreviated by way of a notational system.

389. There are various notational systems commonly used. The one used in this book and throughout most of today's civilization is **algebraic notation**.

390. There are at least four decent reasons for recording chess games:
    (a) to settle disputes (especially in tournament play);
    (b) for chess history and theory (every subject is enhanced by a sense of its own development);
    (c) for personal reasons (how well did you play ten years ago?);
    (d) to read chess books (so that you can expand your knowledge and improve).

391. As many as five items are recorded in the algebraic system:
    (a) the number of the move;
    (b) the symbol of the moving unit (excluding pawns, whose movement is understood by implication);
    (c) the name of the starting square (which is not used in a shortened version);
    (d) whether the unit moves or captures (also not necessary in the shortened form);
    (e) the name of the destination square.

392. One should know something about the **descriptive system** too – not for recording, but to augment the description of certain ideas and actions. It describes the movement of the forces in terms of their names.

393. If a piece starts on the queenside the word "queen" may be appended to it. Thus for White the rook starting on a1 is the queen-rook while the black bishop starting on c8 is the queen-bishop.

394. If a piece starts on the kingside the word "king" may be attached to it. Thus the black rook starting on h8 is the king-rook and the white knight starting on g1 is the king-knight.

395. But you don't need to know any of this to record a game in the algebraic system. For now, it's sufficient that you know that the descriptive system exists.

396. Here are some other abbreviations used in this book which you may find useful in recording a chess game.

Symbol	Meaning
–	moves to
x	captures
...	signifies Black's move when given independently of White's
0-0	castles kingside
0-0-0	castles queenside
+	check
!	good move
!!	very good move
?	questionable move
??	very bad move

397. Earlier we looked at the Fool's Mate. Let's see how that two-move game is recorded in full algebraic notation (Diagrams 135-138).

Diagram 135
f2-f3

Diagram 136
e7-e5

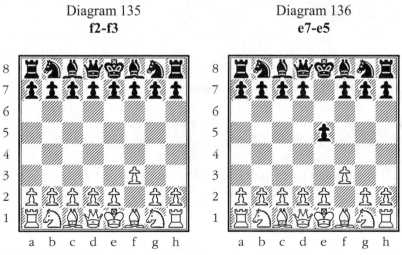

The pawn's symbol is not needed

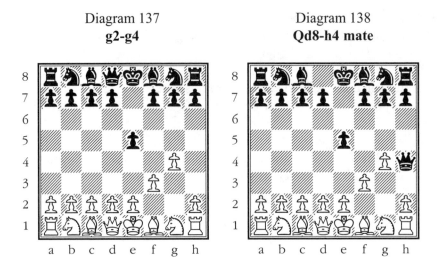

Diagram 137
g2-g4

398. Here's how the game would appear on a score sheet:

No.	White's Move	Black's Move
1.	f2-f3	e7-e5
2.	g2-g4	Qd8-h4 mate

399. Here's how the game would look if it were written in linear form in a book using full algebraic notation: **1. f2-f3 e7-e5 2. g2-g4 Qd8-h4 mate**.

400. Here's how the game would appear if a shortened form of linear notation were used: **1. f3 e5 2. g4 Qh4 mate**.

401. If you wish to record your own games, and haven't got any score sheets, perhaps you could make your own from the above model (of statement 398) and photocopy a certain number of sheets.

402. One final detail concerns **the touch move rule**. If on your turn you touch one of your pieces or pawns you must move it.

403. If you haven't taken your hand off the touched friendly unit you may still have an option where to place it.

404. But once your hand has left the unit the move stands.

405. You don't have to move the unit if it doesn't have a legal move. Instead you can play any other move of your choosing (some tournaments may impose time penalties, but this is not integral to the game).

406. Moreover, if on your turn you touch an enemy unit you must capture it.

407. If different friendly units can make the capture you may be selective.

408. But if none of your pieces or pawns can capture the touched enemy unit you're free to play any other move of your choosing.

409. The only way you can touch a unit and avoid moving it is to announce your intention of adjusting it beforehand. You can say **I adjust** or *ja'doube* if you prefer French.

410. You have now completed another part of the course. You know how to play chess, but you still may not know how to play well. The remaining segments of this book discuss the right things to do. Maybe it's slightly harder. And perhaps it might require a bit more thinking at points. If so, I'm hoping that's a good thing.

411. Certainly try to understand everything you read in *Let's Play Chess*, reviewing as much as necessary and desirable. But if you can't immediately comprehend the point of a particular statement, and you've already invested some time on it, it's okay to move on. You can always get future takes on the same thoughts after you've had more practical experience. And that's what you need to do fairly soon: play some chess so you can try out your new ideas.

Section Thirteen: Winning Material

412. Unless your opponent plays badly it's not likely you'll mate him or her early in the game. If you can't force an immediate mate the game could go on for quite some time. With proper defense, even horribly losing positions can be extended for many moves.

413. In such circumstances it's not expected that you see in your mind all the way to the end of the game. If you could you wouldn't need this book. Maybe I'd be reading your book.

414. From the start of a game you should keep your eyes open for mating opportunities. But the schooled player at first doesn't aim so much for mate. Rather he or she, as we've already seen, plays to get the advantage.

415. As already indicated, various factors determine who has the overall advantage in a chess position, with the easiest factor to understand and evaluate being material.

416. Our opponent doesn't want to give up material for nothing. So the usual trick is to win material by deception and counter-deception.

417. Other than taking for nothing, double attack is the main way to win material.

418. A **double attack** is an aggressive move that menaces the opponent in at least two ways simultaneously.

419. Although there are all kinds of double attacks, usually the concept implies issuing threats to at least two different enemy units.

420. Double attacks are examples of tactics. Two words often confused are strategy and tactics.

421. Strategy refers to an overall plan. It tends to be general and long term.

422. Tactics are the individual operations used to bring about that plan. They tend to be specific and short term.

423. If strategy is what you are going to do, tactics are how you are going to do it.

424. Tactics are the real meat-and-potatoes of a chess game. It could be that as much as three quarters or better of chess play is tactical.

425. There are five main tactical ideas:
   (a) the fork - an attacker threatens to capture two or more defenders;
   (b) the pin - an attacker forces a defender to shield another;
   (c) the skewer - an attacker forces a defender to expose another;
   (d) discovery - an attacker uncovers the attack of another; and
   (e) undermining - an attacker removes or thwarts defense of another.

426. The two most common tactics are forks and pins.

427. The **fork** is a tactic by which one chess unit directly attacks two or more opposing units on the same move.

428. Every unit is capable of giving a fork.

429. Diagram 139 illustrates a knight fork. The knight attacks the black king and queen simultaneously. After Black moves the king to safety the knight captures the queen.

430. Diagram 140 shows a pawn fork. The pawn forks the knight and the rook. If the knight moves, the pawn captures the rook. If the rook moves anywhere but h4, the pawn captures the knight.

Diagram 139
A knight fork

Diagram 140
A pawn fork

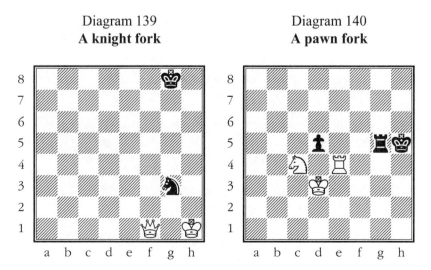

Diagram 141
A bishop fork

Diagram 142
A rook fork

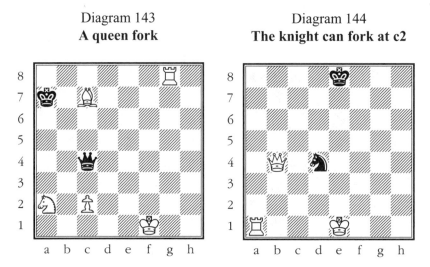

431. Diagram 141 shows a bishop fork. The bishop forks the king, rook and knight. After White gets out of check the bishop will take the rook.

432. Diagram 142 shows a rook fork. The rook forks the king, bishop, knight, and pawn.

433. Diagram 143 shows a queen fork. The queen forks the white king, rook, knight, bishop, and pawn.

434. In Diagram 144 Black to play can fork the king, queen and rook – known as a **family fork** or a **royal fork**. The solution is **Nd4-c2+**. After White gets out of check the knight will capture the queen.

Diagram 143
A queen fork

Diagram 144
The knight can fork at c2

435. In Diagram 145 White's queen can capture the pawn, **Qd1xd5+**, thereby forking the black king and rook. After the king gets out of check the rook will be captured.

436. Forks are easy enough to understand, whereas pins are often slightly harder to grasp.

437. The pin is a tactic that prevents an enemy unit from moving off a line. That is, off a rank, file or diagonal. To do so would expose another unit to capture or an important square to attack along the line of the pin.

Diagram 145
The can queen can fork at d5

438. Pins usually involve at least one attacker and two opposing targets.

439. The attacker and its two enemy targets must all be on the same rank, file, or diagonal. In other words a straight line can be drawn through all three units and/or points of interest.

440. Diagram 146 shows a simple pin and should help you to understand the concept. The rook attacks and threatens the knight along the g-file. Black is unable to move the knight to safety because it shields the king from the rook. Thus the knight is frozen or **pinned** and will be captured next move for free.

Diagram 146
A simple pin

441. In Diagram 146 the situation is described this way: **the rook pins the knight to the king**. Moreover, all three units – the rook and the two enemy targets – line up on the same file.

442. If you want to use your imagination, picture the rook as a straight pin, the knight as a sheet of paper,

The knight is lost

83

and the black king as a bulletin board. This resemblance to a real metal pin partly explains the origin of the word.

443. Only bishops, rooks, and queens – **the line pieces** – can pin.

444. There are two kinds of pins:
(a) absolute pins; and
(b) relative pins.

445. An **absolute pin** is a pin to the king. The pinned unit can't move off the line of the pin.

446. A **relative pin** is a pin to any unit other than the king. The pinned unit can legally move off the line of the pin but it may be undesirable to do so.

Diagram 147
A relative pin

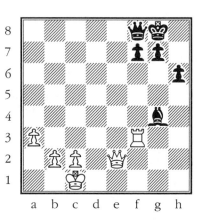

447. Diagram 146 shows an absolute pin. It's illegal for Black to move the knight.

448. Diagram 147 shows a relative pin. The rook can move but that would expose the queen to capture. There are times when sacrificing the queen might be worth it but this is not one of them.

Diagram 148
Black to move

449. A useful pinning idea occurs in Diagram 148 with Black to play. It starts with the rook moving to e8, pinning the bishop to the king, as shown in Diagram 148a.

450. To protect the bishop White must play d2-d3. That saves the bishop but it remains pinned (Diagram 149).

451. Naturally, Black will not take the bishop (worth three pawns) since White's pawn then takes the rook (worth five pawns). That's not a good deal, with Black losing two pawns in value. But there's no need to take the bishop. It's pinned and can't run away.

452. So if it's not immediately desirable to capture a pinned unit, what should one do to it?

453. The answer is to attack the pinned unit once again, especially with something of little value. Thus

Diagram 148a
After pinning the bishop

we see in Diagram 150 that Black plays the f-pawn to f5 and the bishop is lost. The pawn will take the bishop next move.

Diagram 149
After defending the bishop

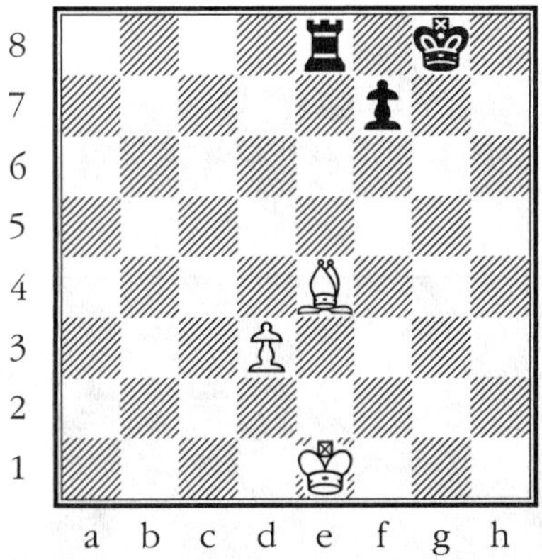

Diagram 150
White's bishop is lost

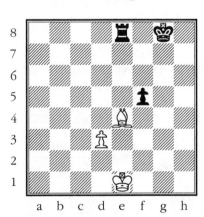

454. As a rule of thumb try to pin your opponent's pieces.

455. Avoid putting your own pieces in pins.

456. And once you've pinned an enemy unit don't necessarily take it. Make sure capturing it is to your advantage.

457. If it's not desirable to take the pinned unit right away, keep the pin. Then try to increase the pressure against the pinned unit, especially by attacking it again and again until defense becomes difficult or impossible.

458. Even if the pressure against a pinned unit doesn't lead to material gain, maintenance of the pin reduces your opponent's options. That in itself can constitute an advantage.

459. Some pins can be broken.

460. There are four ways to try to break a pin:
   (a) moving the pinned unit away and accepting the consequences (this can only happen if the pin is a relative one);
   (b) blocking the line between the pinning and the pinned unit;
   (c) moving the back target away, ending the pin;
   (d) or simply capturing the pinning unit.

461. Diagram 151 shows a relative pin that can be broken safely. With the turn Black can move the rook out of the pin, checking at c1. White must get out of check, moving the king to g2, allowing Black's queen time to move to safety, say to d1 (Diagram 152). The result is that both the rook and queen are saved, the pin is ended, and Black is starting to muster counter-threats.

Diagram 151
**Black can move the pinned unit
with check**

Diagram 152
After 1...Rc1+ 2. Kg2 Qd1

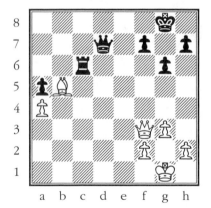
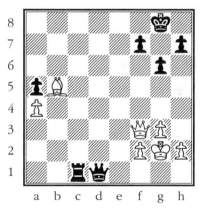

462. Another way to break a pin is by interposing a friendly unit between the pinned unit and the one to which it's pinned. In Diagram 153 Black's knight is pinned by the rook to its king. The knight is also subject to capture by White's pawn. Yet the knight can be saved.

463. The key is to retreat the bishop to e6, giving check to White's king (Diagram 154). At e6 the bishop also provides additional shielding to the black king, with the knight no longer being pinned.

Diagram 153
Black can save the knight

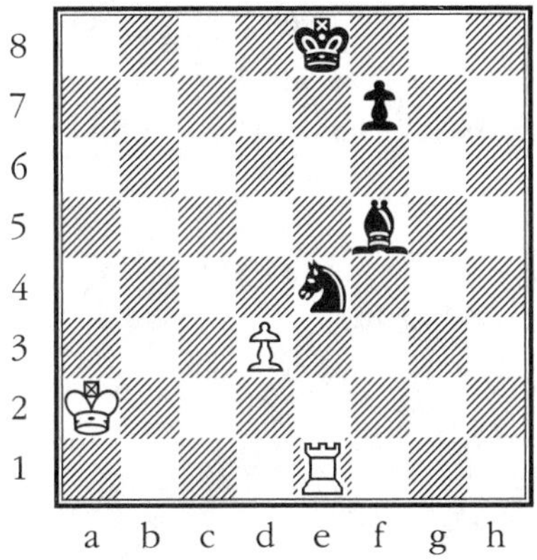

Diagram 154
After 1...Bf5-e6+

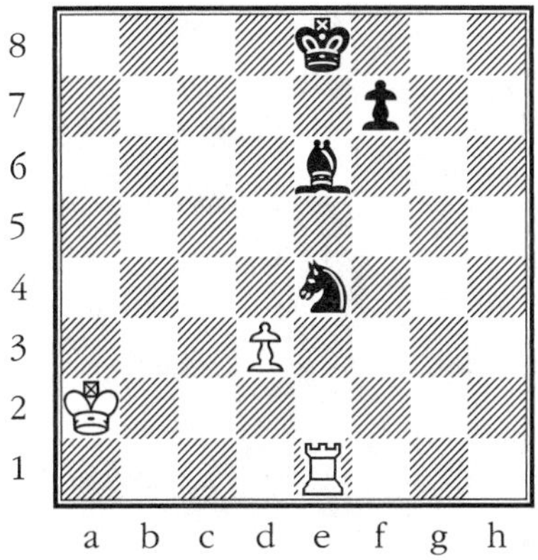

464. Once the white king moves to safety (say to b2) the knight will be able to move to safety as well (say to f6), as in Diagram 155, and Black has avoided loss of material.

465. Black gained time by checking with the bishop. You can **gain time** in various ways, such as taking fewer moves to complete a transaction or by avoiding unnecessary moves. And there are still other ways to gain time as well.

466. In the context of Diagram 153 Black gains time by **giving check**. This forces White to waste a move in defense of the king. Thus White isn't yet able to capture the knight.

Diagram 155
The knight has escaped the pin

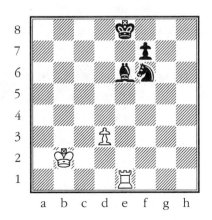

87

467. Still, gaining time can be an elusive concept, and sometimes giving a check can lose time, especially if the opponent can answer the check with a strong move that improves the situation for the defender.

468. So don't just give a check merely because you can. Only do so if it advances your position or fits in with your plans, the same criteria you'd apply to the consideration of any other move.

469. An example of moving the back target of a pin with a gain of time is illustrated in Diagram 156. White's bishop is pinning the knight to its king in an absolute pin. Although the knight is guarded by a pawn, the white pawn on d5 is threatening to take the knight with material gain.

Diagram 156
Black's knight seems to be lost

Diagram 157
Castling has saved the day

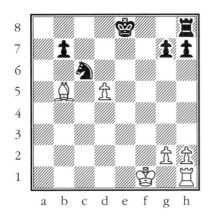
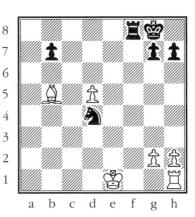

470. But it's Black's move, and before White gets a chance to capture the pinned knight Black can castle – **with check!** After White gets out of check (say moving the king to e1) the knight will be free to move to safety (say to d4), as in Diagram 157.

471. There are other standard tactics, but pins and forks are the most significant because they impact almost every game. But that's enough tactics.

472. The sections on mating patterns and winning material both demonstrate the powers of the pieces and pawns. There are other factors in chess besides mate and material and we shall come to more of them shortly. For now, look for double attacks, especially pins and forks. And if you can't find them, set them up. I hear that's the real fun.

Section Fourteen: Principles

473. In chess first you learn the rules (how to play) and then the principles (how to play well).

474. Principles are general truths that advise actions to take or avoid.

475. Rules are laws that must be obeyed.

476. You can disregard or violate principles; you can't disregard or violate rules.

477. Yet principles should be followed unless there's a definite reason for defying or marginalizing them.

478. Some confusion may ensue because of common phrasing, such as use of the idiom "rule of thumb." In chess a **rule of thumb** is like a principle. It too refers to a general truth based on experience. It can be a guideline, maxim or piece of advice, but it's clearly not to be taken as a law of the game.

479. The difference between rules and principles can be illustrated with regard to castling. The rule is that you move the king two squares toward the rook and then bring the rook to the other side of the king. The principle is that you should **aim to castle early in the game**.

480. The rule is always true; the principle is usually or often true.

481. To apply a principle you need to know something about your situation. This requires that you first analyze the position to see who stands better and why.

482. Once you've done that you can ask questions to elicit information. You might ask something like: are there any principles that apply to my situation?

483. Obviously, you don't have to put it that way. You can go with your own language and phrasing to trigger pertinent reasoning.

484. Principles are helpful when you're confused and uncertain. You might ask: What does the principle suggest I do in this kind of position?

485. This doesn't mean you should follow the principle you think of blindly. Rather use it to point the way. There may be a relevant exception or the principle might not really apply. So you still must analyze before finalizing plans and deciding on your next move.

486. Remember that a generality can jumpstart the thinking process but never replace it.

487. From here on, in all you chess doings, you're likely to encounter new and exciting chess principles. Learn them, use them, master them, but don't become discouraged if they elude you or seem paradoxical. Indeed, there are times when the very opposite of a principle is the way to go. But this is a matter of experience, and there's no substitute for that.

Section Fifteen: The Opening

488. The opening is the beginning part of a chess game. It usually lasts ten to fifteen moves, though the tendency today is to extend opening study as far as reasonably possible, especially with the help of computers and specialized software.

489. There is no agreement on the best opening move, but for beginners playing White I recommend moving the e-pawn two squares ahead (e2-e4).

490. White starts with a slight advantage known as **the initiative**.

491. Having the initiative enables White to push and drive the play.

492. In most chess positions, though not all, it's usually better to attack than defend. In battle the first strike is often decisive.

493. In chess the attacker has a practical advantage. Even after making a mistake there's a chance to recover since defenders are generally unprepared to switch to attack.

494. But if the defender errs the result often has more serious immediate consequences and might even lose the game. One reason for this is that the attacker has typically anticipated the possibility of error and is geared to exploit the situation.

495. You have the initiative if you can direct the course of events to force the action.

496. The attacker directs the action and the defender reacts to it.

497. Yet while the attacker has the initiative the defender tries to take it away.

498. In theory, but not necessarily in practice, it seems the attacker is trying to win and the defender is trying to draw.

499. In a way the defender is trying to become the attacker.

500. If you have a real attack, and therefore a true initiative, you have control over the position.

501. That's what the chess battle is really about: **gaining control**.

502. Both players want to seize command so that they can play freely and put the other player in a situation requiring compliance.

503. Some experienced players disregard theory and try to win with both White and Black. With Black they blend defense and counterattack, leading to sharp, tense, complicated play. To win they take calculated chances and are willing to risk some defeats hoping for many more victories.

504. It's important to grasp that an opening line is not just about what you want. Rather it reflects an interaction between you and your opponent. Surely you're striving to achieve your own aims. But your opponent has plans too.

505. Whatever you attempt to do your opponent will try to anticipate, frustrate, and thwart. You may even be allowed to get what you want. That is, your opponent may have seen more than you and has set a surprise ambush.

506. The point is that you shouldn't just play a set of opening moves regardless of likely opposing responses. That's a sure way to lose before you actually do.

507. Although there may not be a best opening move there's a best opening plan: to develop and play for the center.

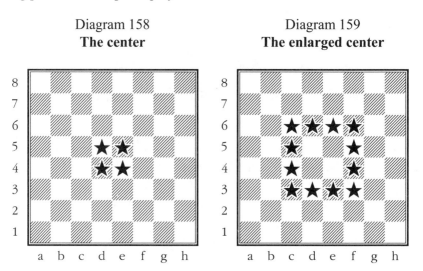

Diagram 158
The center

Diagram 159
The enlarged center

508. To **play for the center** means to occupy, guard, and influence the squares in the very center of the board: e4, e5, d4, and d5 (Diagram 158).

509. The squares that surround the center are also important (Diagram 159).

510. From the start both sides actively fight for the center. One way to do this is by occupying central squares.

511. You should try to install your pieces securely in the center for at least five reasons:
  (a) to prepare for action;
  (b) to restrict your opponent;
  (c) to increase mobility;
  (d) to gain space;
  (e) to get closer to the opponent.

512. To prepare for action: pieces in the center can move to either side of the board more quickly and easily than they can from anywhere else. You're more prepared for the fortunes of war when your pieces occupy ideal posts in the center.

513. To restrict your opponent: pieces in the center tend to impede the coordination of the opponent's forces. A nicely stationed central force presents an imposing barrier.

514. To increase mobility: pieces in or near the center tend to be more mobile. They have more squares to which they can move and therefore more options and more primary and secondary targets.

515. To gain space: occupying the center usually provides more room behind the lines for maneuvering, and spatial gain corresponds to increases in opportunity.

516. One proviso, however, is not to advance so far and quickly that you overextend yourself, allowing serious incursions into your own territory.

517. To get closer to the opponent: from a secure central base friendly pieces don't have far to go before launching lethal attacks and threats.

518. Every type of piece except the rook enjoys greater mobility as it approaches the center. The knight needs the center the most and the rook the least.

519. More significant for the rook is to find open or partially open files leading to the enemy position. Since the rook is just as effective from far away, it doesn't need the center to invade the opponent's camp.

520. Central occupation, however, doesn't guarantee central control. Since no piece or pawn guards itself, the square it occupies may still be insecure.

521. It's an odd thing, but after a piece moves it then guards the square it occupied on the previous move.

522. In trying to occupy the center aim to do so with protection. Either support the region first, then occupy it, or occupy it and then quickly back up that occupation.

523. As a rule of thumb, whenever you have time, and can do so without incurring problems, overprotect your advanced central points. This way, in case you have an oversight, or your opponent begins diverting action, you're still covered and prepared.

524. Besides occupying and guarding the center you can also influence it. A chief way to do this is by driving away opposing pieces. A move away from the center, say on the wing, may actually affect the center by getting rid of an enemy unit that directly bears on it.

525. There are other approaches to the center, both direct and indirect, but for now focus mainly on the importance of occupying and guarding it. That will take you pretty far, until experience takes you a little further.

Section Sixteen: Development

526. Victory in chess usually depends on who gets there first with the most.

527. In the opening you should mobilize all your forces as soon as you can. This is **the principle of development**.

528. To develop a piece is to increase its potential by moving it from its original square to a more useful one or by moving a pawn out of its way.

529. The two great opening principles of centralization and development actually merge into a more comprehensive one: **develop your pieces toward the center**.

530. Try to develop a new piece on each move.

531. Try to move each piece once before moving any piece twice, unless circumstances require otherwise or an opportunity presents itself. In those instances moving a piece several times may make sense.

532. Don't develop mechanically. Develop each piece to its best available square.

533. If early in a game you need two moves or more to reach an ideal square, corroborate your thinking with concrete analysis before commencing the deployment.

534. In the opening you might not have the time to move the same piece on consecutive turns without losing the initiative and possibly more.

535. Try to make pawn moves that contribute to development. Pawn moves should open lines for new pieces to come out while they also guard important squares.

536. Avoid unnecessary pawn moves.

537. Actually, avoid all unnecessary moves of any kind.

538. Stay away from pawn moves that engender serious weakness. Particularly avoid creating weak spots around your king. Your opponent may aim to place pieces on those squares and you might not be able to prevent that or drive them away.

539. In the opening the two best pawns for a newcomer to move are the d- and e-pawns (the two center pawns).

540. Even though you may have seen strong players do it, don't experiment by moving pawns away from the center, such as wing pawns to develop bishops on the flank. This idea and related ones are perfectly good but harder for the beginner to grasp initially.

541. Strong players tend to know what they're doing. You may not. So as a rule of thumb, if you don't fully appreciate an atypical opening pawn move, don't make it – at least not until experience and skill can render it intelligible and practical.

542. Try to move the center pawns two squares each to form a **classical pawn center**.

543. But don't robotically do this. Make sure the tactics work out adequately.

544. Also take note that such advances are more practicable for White. By going second, and being a move behind, Black has a harder time of it.

545. Usually Black can't advance both center pawns two squares early on without incurring undue risk and likely disadvantage.

546. In Diagram 160 the white pawns occupy two central squares (d4 and e4) and guard the other ones (d5 and e5). In addition the d-pawn is already protected by the queen.

547. With such a center White is able to develop all the pieces without having to move another pawn.

548. If Black doesn't interfere all the white pieces can be developed in seven or eight moves from the position of Diagram 160.

Diagram 160
A classical pawn center

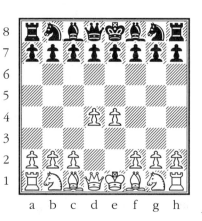

96

549. A sample variation would be Ng1-f3, Bf1-c4, Nb1-c3, Bc1-f4, 0-0 (castles kingside), Qd1-d3, Ra1-d1, and Rf1-e1. That's eight moves and White has developed all the pieces, as shown in Diagram 161, with only one piece (the king-rook) having moved more than once. It moved twice.

550. The same essential setup can be achieved in one move less by castling queenside. That possibility is illustrated in Diagram 162.

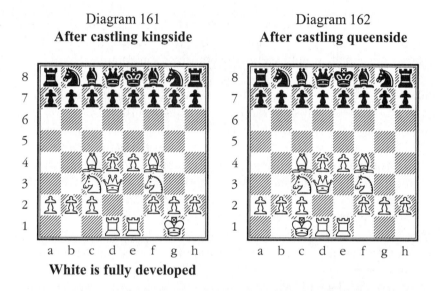

Diagram 161
After castling kingside

Diagram 162
After castling queenside

White is fully developed

551. Usually development is completed by moving all the pieces and castling (remember that pawns are not pieces).

552. The order of development can be important.

553. It's a good idea to develop the minor pieces first (knights and bishops).

554. There's a maxim that advocates developing knights before bishops. The argument is that knights should be developed first because they need more time to reach the enemy. To be effective they must be up close, so they need a head start.

555. The contention is that each knight basically has one good developing move, regardless what the opponent does. That is, knights should be developed toward the enlarged center.

556. Thus most of the time White's knights move to f3 and c3, and much of the time Black's knights move to f6 and c6.

557. Indeed, a knight on f3, c3, f6, or c6 attacks eight different squares. On its starting square a knight assails only three squares.

558. But for White and Black these developments are not automatically best. It always depends on what's actually happening.

559. Unlike the knight the bishop may have a few good developing moves, depending what the opponent does, and therefore it makes sense to delay a bishop's development until seeing the opponent's intentions.

560. Bishops should be developed to open diagonals (diagonals not blocked by friendly pawns). A bishop can't penetrate its own forces.

561. So the theory is fairly clear. Since early in the game you're more certain where to place your knights, you can put them out there (say on squares c3 and f3) with less commitment. However, if on any side of the board you develop the bishop before the knight, you may be revealing information prematurely and unnecessarily.

562. But there are an incredible number of practical exceptions to the principle of developing knights before bishops. On a solid chunk of occasions knights are developed to their second rank or even to the edge (a rook-file), depending on circumstances.

563. Furthermore, it's often useful or necessary to develop a bishop before developing any knights.

564. So while the guideline "knights before bishops" has some minimal value, it shouldn't be followed too religiously. Play so perfunctorily and the "principle" may help you lose more games than it helps you win.

565. Since kingside castling is more usual chess pundits often suggest a specific order of development.

566. They recommend developing the kingside minor pieces before developing the queenside ones, especially if you have White, so that kingside castling is expedited.

567. One approach consistent with this is developing the kingside knight, then the kingside bishop, then the queenside knight, and then the queenside bishop. (Remember the queenside is made up of the a-, b-, c-, and d-files, while the kingside consists of the e-, f-, g-, and h-files.)

568. However, since the second player is under fire from White, it may be more difficult for Black to conform to an imposed development sequence. It might not be feasible for Black to develop both kingside minor pieces before developing any queenside ones, since Black must find specific moves that meet White's pressure and threats.

569. For White this idea also tends to be more true in double king-pawn openings (1. e2-e4 e7-e5). There are many other openings for which the concept has little significance.

570. Another aspect of development concerns castling. Castling is usually a developing move because it enables a rook to come to the center. It gets the king out of the way and enables the rooks to connect so they can support each other.

571. But castling can be a defensive move too. It gets the king out of the uncovered center, where pawns are likely to have been moved and exchanged.

572. Castling can place the king behind a sheltering wall of pawns, if you haven't moved the pawns on the castling side.

573. Generally, after castling, try not to move the pawns in front of your king. It's usually a good idea to keep a fence of protection between yourself and the enemy.

574. For some the word *castling* recalls the idea of medieval nobleman fortifying themselves in real castles. For others it's just a move in chess.

575. The principle is: castle early.

576. But here too the principle is coarsely put. You wouldn't want to castle into a mating attack.

577. So rather than "castle early" a modified principle seems more prudent: **prepare to castle early**. This way you're ready for castling but have options.

578. Rooks should be developed to **open files** (files unoccupied by pawns), **half-open files** (files occupied just by enemy pawns), or files that are more likely to open (files with advanced friendly pawns that may soon be exchanged for enemy pawns).

579. In Diagram 163 the c-file is open, the e-file is half open for White, and the g-file is half open for Black. All the other files are closed for both sides.

580. The maxim expressing the principle is: **rooks belong on open files**.

581. Rooks stationed on open and half-open files can attack and penetrate the enemy position, whereas rooks on closed files can't attack the opponent at all since friendly and enemy pawns obstruct the way.

582. Thus a related principle is: rooks belong on half-open files. On half-open files rooks can attack enemy pawns and exert pressure.

583. In Diagram 164 the white rooks should move to the half-open b- and e-files while the black rooks should move to the half-open d- and a-files.

584. Try to control open lines (the files, ranks, and diagonals with no pawns in the way).

585. Rooks need open files and ranks. Bishops need open diagonals. Queens need open files, ranks, and diagonals.

Diagram 163	Diagram 164
Open and half-open files	**Where to place the rooks**

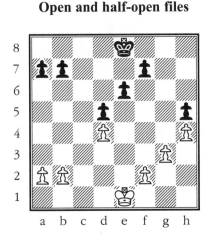
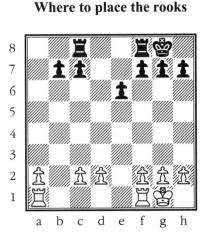

586. Queens, rooks, and bishops are long-range pieces. They work effectively from a distance.

587. Lines blocked by pawns are **closed** since pawns can't conveniently be moved off the line. Lines blocked by pieces are semi-open, since pieces generally can be moved off the line if necessary or desired. Control the open lines and you control the gateways to the opposing position.

588. In the opening try to develop with threats. As a reminder, a threat is an attack that if ignored would bring advantage to the attacker.

589. Thus threats force or essentially force responses. As you shouldn't ignore threats to your person you shouldn't ignore threats to your position.

590. As previously indicated, threats tend to gain time. The player threatened usually must expend at least a move to cope with it.

591. If you gain time you gain moves. If you lose time you lose moves.

592. An attractive beginning for the newcomer is to bring out the queen, hoping to steal pawns and pieces.

593. You may wish to bring out the queen early, but try not to do so without careful consideration. It's easy to think merely of the queen's power and not of the possibility of losing it.

594. Even if you don't lose it you may be forced into serious concessions saving it.

595. A queen developed too early is unprotected and subject to attack. It's value compels moving it to safety practically every time it's attacked, unless the attack comes from the opposing queen.

596. A lone queen without backing can't necessarily do much anyway, considering it might have to contend with an army of opposing pieces and pawns. As in a play a supporting cast is necessary.

597. You could try to keep your queen stationed centrally, but failure is guaranteed to result. In Diagram 165, for instance, the black queen is exposed. The position arose after 1. e2-e4 d7-d5 2. e4xd5 Qd8xd5. White should try to attack the queen by developing a new piece.

Diagram 165
Black's queen is subject to attack

Diagram 166
After 3. Nb1-c3

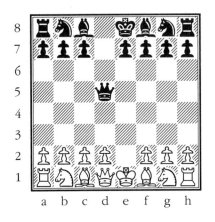

598. In Diagram 166 White gains time on the queen by attacking and threatening it with the queen-knight, **3. Nb1-c3**. Black will have to waste a tempo getting the queen to safety.

599. Black should move the queen to safety, say to a5 or to d8. But let's say, for point of illustration, that Black tries to keep the queen in the center with **3...Qd5-d4?** (Diagram 167).

600. But this a bad decision, enabling White to develop the other knight, again with a threat to the black queen. Thus **4. Ng1-f3** (Diagram 168) gains time.

Diagram 167
After 3...Qd5-d4?

Diagram 168
After 4. Ng1-f3

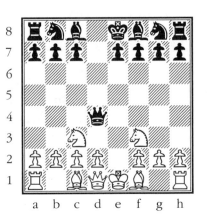

Diagram 169
After 4...Qd4-c5?

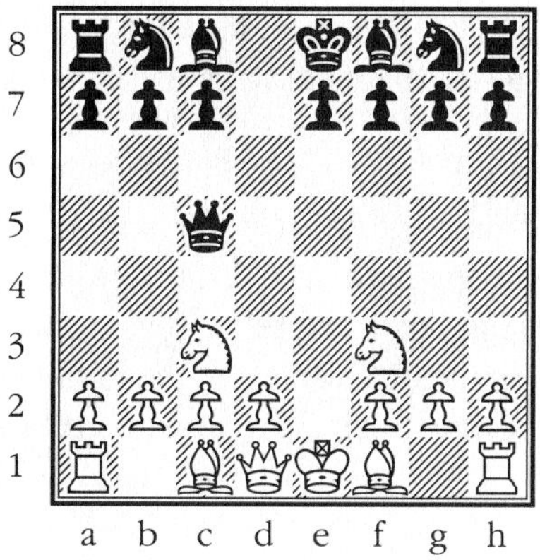

Diagram 170
After 5. d2-d4

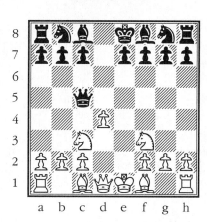

601. Notice that together the white knights guard the entire four squares in the middle. Black should beat a retreat to safety and avoid further embarrassment.

602. Suppose Black continues with the same jejune idea of keeping the queen near the center by playing **4...Qd4-c5?** (Diagram 169).

603. White then has another useful move: **5. d2-d4** (Diagram 170). That attacks the queen and opens further lines for development and attack. Once again Black will have to waste a tempo moving the queen to safety.

Diagram 171
After 5...Qc5-c6

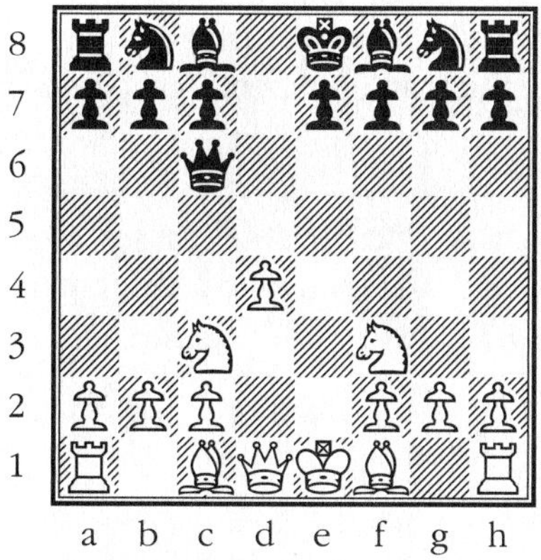

Diagram 172
Pinning and winning the queen

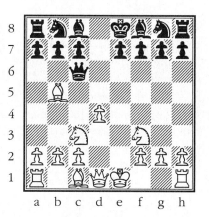

604. Suppose Black now replies by moving the queen back, **5...Qc5-c6??**. This is a blunder that loses the queen (Diagram 171).

605. White now develops a new piece and pins the queen, **6. Bf1-b5** (Diagram 172). The queen can't move off the a4-e8 diagonal without exposing the king to check.

606. White was able to make four developing moves at Black's expense (three piece moves and one pawn move that opened lines). While this game is not very sensible, it points out how treacherous it can be to rely on early queen sorties. I can't tell you how many games I've actually seen played just as irrationally. It can't be said enough: **don't bring the queen out too early**.

607. One question is: what's meant by coming out too early? That question can only be answered in context.

608. If your opponent's queen comes out ostensibly early, try to attack it.

609. But don't just attack the enemy queen haphazardly; try to build, improve, and develop your position at the same time.

610. You may be tempted to violate the principles simply because you're playing another beginner. You may think that other beginners are too weak to take advantage of risky, inexact, or even knowingly incorrect play.

611. Experienced players don't take such chances – a mark in their favor (there are others). They always try to play their best regardless of their opponents.

612. Think about it. If your opponent is truly weak he or she is just as likely to play a good move as a bad one. Such an opponent's response is totally unpredictable.

613. At this point, even though you may have questions, take away from the preceding analysis the importance of centralization and development. Those ideas should impel you deeper into the theory of the game, at least to the next section.

Section Seventeen: Chess Thinking

614. In the study of any subject problems may arise that can't be answered immediately. Especially in chess some situations and concepts require considerable experience before they can be properly understood.

615. Be practical. You don't have to understand every detail to play chess well. Assimilate what you can from an idea, and even if you grasp only a portion or aspect of it, try to put that to use. As you gain experience the idea will become clearer and you should gain more command over it.

616. There are many facets to chess study. More important than memorizing some specific facts is knowing how to examine a chess position.

617. A critical evaluation of a chess position is called an **analysis**.

618. To analyze a chess position is to break it down into its key elements to determine who stands better.

619. Once you size up who stands better and why you can choose a plan appropriate to that assessment.

620. Every position suggests a suitable plan, and often there are a number of approaches that might succeed. Your aim should be to formulate a strategy consistent with your needs and goals.

621. An intelligent plan should maximize your chances to win while minimizing the likelihood of loss.

622. Among the various factors evaluated in an analysis are **material**, **mobility** (often under the code name **space**), development (appearing as **time**), **pawn structure**, and **king safety**.

623. These factors are further differentiated. There are permanent (lasting, long-term) advantages and impermanent (temporary, short-term) advantages.

624. Material and pawn structure are the more tangible elements. You can see them and even count them.

625. You don't necessarily have to exploit tangibly more permanent advantages right away, since they're likely to be there for some time. You might still be able to capitalize on them much later.

626. Time and space are more intangible elements. They are harder to evaluate numerically, if at all. Therefore they have to be appreciated differently.

627. If you don't capitalize on intangibles soon enough they're likely to dissipate.

628. For instance, if you're ahead in development, even by several tempi, your opponent will eventually catch up if you do nothing with your superiority.

629. There are five basic analytic evaluations:
(a) White stands better (White has more winning chances than Black);
(b) Black stands better (Black has more winning chances than White);
(c) The game is even or roughly so (both sides have equal chances of winning);
(d) White is winning;
(e) Black is winning.

630. Most analyses are impelled by calculations, which are strings of intention and expectation: your moves and your opponent's likely replies.

631. The action of determining variations of calculation falls under the rubric of **looking ahead**.

632. A natural question is: how far ahead (in your mind) should you look?

633. Most of the time you don't have to look more than a few moves ahead. Trying to look beyond that may be unnecessary and impractical.

634. It can be unnecessary when it's possible to make a clear determination after just a few moves. It can be impractical when there are too many variations to consider and the resulting positions are terribly unclear.

635. Some positions are easy to see through and calculate, especially when your opponent has few ways to respond to your projected moves.

636. Other positions are very complex, with the opponent having too many apparently plausible ways of responding. You'd probably be wasting mental and emotional resources trying to extend your analysis in those instances.

637. As a rule of thumb you should always try to look at least three half moves ahead: that is, you should consider your next move, your opponent's likely response, and how you intend to follow up on that. If you can do that, see three half moves ahead, at least you're playing chess.

638. For the most part good players play by the principles and place great emphasis on the laws of likelihood.

639. In chess ninety-nine percent of the unforeseen possibilities can be dealt with as they arise — if you have command and understanding over the position. Therefore it wastes time and effort to look needlessly deep into most positions.

640. You should employ a chess version of Occam's Razor and never look further ahead than necessary.

641. The theory and logic of chess ensure that if you have a winning position, regardless what the opponent does, you can ultimately convert that advantageous setup into mate. You still may have to find some very good moves along the way, but at least you know the moves are there to be found. This may not be a comfort, but it's a thought that can surely be relied on with some confidence.

642. Although I can't prove to you that the principles of chess work in the main, centuries of chess history confirm that they do. Actually, in many chess positions, it's easier to disprove an idea than to prove it.

643. For now, however, you should simply accept that the principles work so that you can move on and garner more experience. That is, until you've lost an awful lot of chess games, trying to prove your ideas and disprove your opponent's.

644. Actually, since every game is a learning experience, the more games you lose the better player you're likely to become – up to a point.

645. Once you accept that a winning position should lead to mate, you need to acquire the technique to convert those situations into actual victory.

646. Though some winning advantages are easy to convert, others can require considerable patience and accuracy.

647. Material advantages of a piece or more are reasonably easy enough to execute. However, at first you may have trouble capitalizing on only the most overwhelming superiority.

648. Masters usually can win with as little as an extra pawn, but at first you may not be able to win with an extra queen.

649. Nonmaterial factors can be equally important but are harder to take advantage of. Nevertheless, you should be able to sense that a powerful attack against a defenseless king, a great lead in development, and a vast superiority in space are desirable factors. You probably just don't have the technique to win consistently with these advantages.

650. Technique refers to the methodical and skillful handling of certain tasks.

651. Technique comes through as quality and quantity.

652. You can have better technique and more technique. You can have worse technique and less technique. Everyone has technique, but no two players have the same technique.

653. Since technique is determined by experience and acquired skill I recommend that you start testing yourself regularly against superior opposition. That's a great way to improve and augment your technique.

654. Serious players never stop learning. They constantly observe the play of others. They read chess books and try to solve problems (sometimes the same ones over and over). And after losing they appreciate the value of examining that very game with their opponent.

655. Remember that at every stage you should expect to encounter problems likely to be beyond your present status and comfort level. That's an aspect of the game's challenge. Try your best to solve those problems, but if you still don't quite come up with satisfactory answers, just keep playing and learning. All you probably need is more experience. Fortunately, chess can be enjoyed at all levels, and that's a certainty.

Section Eighteen: An Actual Game

656. It's now time to consider another short chess game. In our particular example the white moves are played by an imaginary chess expert and the black by a typical beginner. Try to follow the moves, alternatives, and explanations as closely as you can, but don't get bogged down on small things. Since you must have an overall picture before you can understand some particular points, play through the entire game to get an overview. That's where important truths may often be found, if there's any to find.

657. White begins with **1. e2-e4** (Diagram 173).

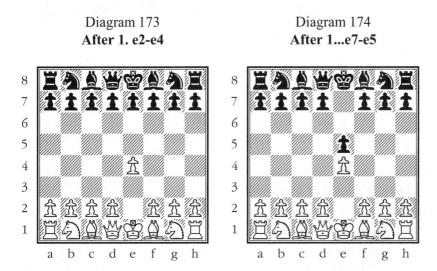

Diagram 173
After 1. e2-e4

Diagram 174
After 1...e7-e5

658. In your own games you should also consider making this opening move because it leads to positions that are easier to understand. The pawn guards a central square (d5) and opens the way for White's queen and bishop. Bobby Fischer once joked that the move 1. e2-e4 was "best by test." Perhaps it wasn't a joke.

659. For similar reasons Black responds **1...e7-e5** (Diagram 174).

660. Now both sides have a share of the center and can develop the same pieces, but White still has the initiative.

661. White continues **2. Ng1-f3** (Diagram 175), developing a new piece and threatening the black e-pawn.

Diagram 175
After 2. Ng1-f3

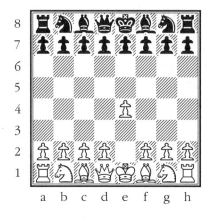

Diagram 176
If Black had played 2...Nb8-c6

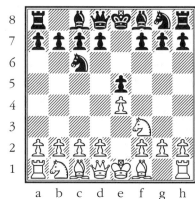

662. An excellent way for Black to protect the e-pawn is 2...Nb8-c6 (Diagram 176), and this also develops a piece toward the center.

663. But Black doesn't play 2...Nb8-c6. (The game itself is a construct, so don't confuse what "could have happened" with what "did.")

664. Another reasonable response would have been 2...d7-d6 (Diagram 177), solidly protecting the e-pawn and opening the diagonal of the light-squared bishop. This is known as Philidor's Defense, named after a great French player of the eighteenth century.

Diagram 177
If Black had played 2...d7-d6

Diagram 178
After 2...f7-f6?

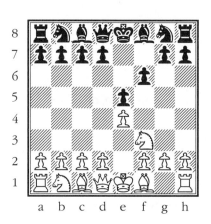

665. But Black doesn't play that either. Instead he or she plays the questionable **2...f7-f6?** (Diagram 178). Remember that a question mark after a move means the move is a mistake. But you probably knew that already.

666. This move is bad because:

(a) it doesn't contribute to development (no new piece can come out after it);

(b) it blocks f6, depriving the black king-knight of its best square;

(c) it weakens the position of the black king (it now will be possible to attack the king along the e8-h5 diagonal);

(d) it enables White to prevent Black from castling kingside (White can post the king-bishop on c4 and guard g8).

667. White now weighs a piece sacrifice, trying to take advantage of the weakened position of the black king. Even though the e-pawn is guarded, White decides to take it anyway by **3. Nf3xe5** (Diagram 180). Basically, a **sacrifice** is the offer of material for some other kind of advantage. Should White be sacrificing without concrete and definite compensation? In this case White gets an attack, but probably a safer but clearly good way to continue would be 3. d2-d4 (Diagram 179).

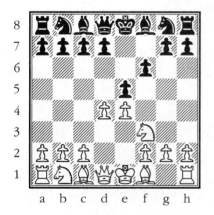

Diagram 179
White could have tried 3. d2-d4

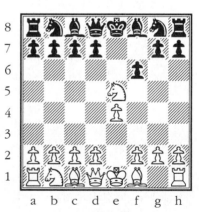

Diagram 180
After 3. Nf3xe5

The move White actually played

668. You are not expected to determine White's moves in this game (especially White's third move, which is somewhat risky and not objectively best). Nevertheless, I hope you stay focused and try to understand the moves after they're explained. But even more important than understanding the moves is sensing what a chess game is all about – feeling the give and take of battle. You'll want to incorporate that spirit into your own games, to put yourself in a position to experience, learn, and win some exhilarating chess games.

669. Black is faced with a difficult decision – to take the knight or not?

670. Let's say Black tries very hard to analyze the position, but still can't decide what to do. Let's say he or she thinks: "If I take the knight, I may be falling into a trap; but if I don't take the knight, I have allowed White to capture one of my pawns for free."

671. In situations analogous to that of statement 670 (when the move isn't clear) try to determine the most practical course of action.

672. In our specific case the most practical course of action is to take the knight because Black can't determine why the sacrifice is offered. That puts the burden on White to prove that the sacrifice is sound.

673. Rely on your own powers. If you can't see the point of a particular move, assume one doesn't exist.

674. If you rely on your own powers either of two good things will happen: you'll be right, or you'll be wrong and your opponent will teach you something!

675. An old chess maxim has it that the best way to refute a sacrifice is to accept it. Of course the maxim doesn't take into account times when accepting the sacrifice loses by force, if that outcome can be foreseen.

676. To learn how to play chess well you should be willing to take chances, which means you have to be prepared to accept some losses.

677. In our particular game Black takes the knight and learns some-

Diagram 181
After 3...f6xe5

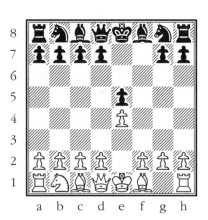

thing! Black continues **3...f6xe5** (Diagram 181).

678. Now that the knight is off the diagonal of the white queen, White is able to play **4. Qd1-h5+** (Diagram 182).

679. Whether White's sacrifice is sound or not, at least there's an immediate point to it: White is forking both the black king and the e5-pawn. Moreover, White senses the possibility of a burgeoning attack.

680. In general **don't sacrifice without good reason**.

681. Now the black king can be shielded with 4...g7-g6 (Diagram 183), but that would allow White to give a new fork by 5. Qh5xe5+ (Diagram 184), winning the rook on h8 after Black gets out of check.

Diagram 182
After 4. Qd1-h5+

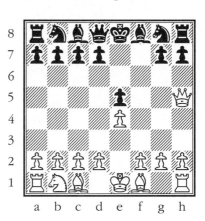

682. So Black didn't play 4...g7-g6 and instead decided to weather the storm and move the king, giving up the right to castle. Black plays **4...Ke8-e7** (Diagram 185).

Diagram 183
If Black had played 4...g7-g6

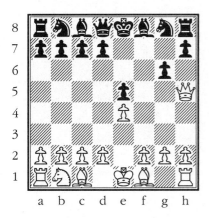

Diagram 184
**White would have played
4. Qh5xe5+**

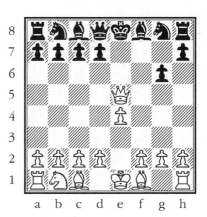

Diagram 185
After 4...Ke8-e7

Diagram 186
After 5. Qh5xe5+

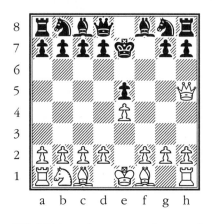
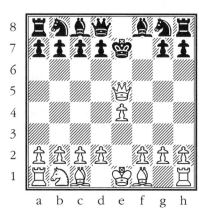

683. White wins a second pawn for the sacrificed knight and continues to attack the black king by **5. Qh5xe5+** (Diagram 186).

684. Black has only one move to get out of check, and that's **5...Ke7-f7** (Diagram 187).

685. The badly exposed black king should be attacked as much as possible. White has five reasonable moves to check the black king: four by the queen (from d5, h5, f4, and f5) and one by the bishop from c4.

686. Instead of wasting time by attacking with the same piece (the queen)

Diagram 187
After 5...Ke7-f7

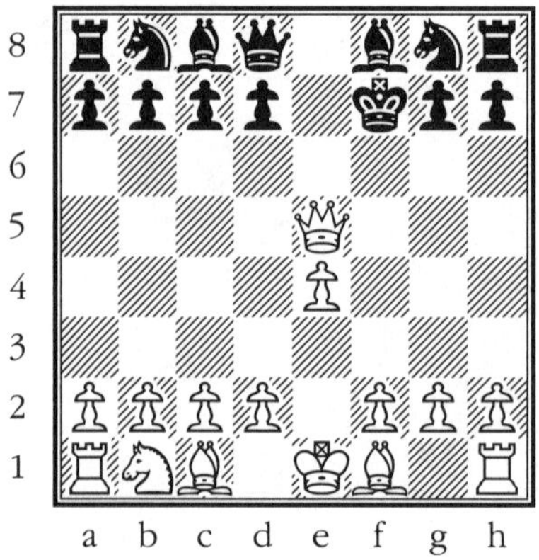

Diagram 188
After 6. Bf1-c4+

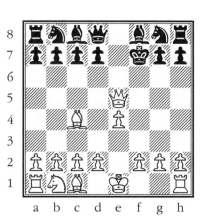

White opts to check with the bishop, thereby bringing a new piece into play. So White plays **6. Bf1-c4+** (Diagram 188).

687. When you attack mobilize as many different pieces as you can. In our present game it seems foolish to have the white queen do what can be done just as well by the bishop. It can give a pesky check too.

688. Black could block the check by 6...d7-d5 (Diagram 189) but that would give back another pawn after 7. Bc4xd5+ (Diagram 190).

Diagram 189
**If Black had played
6...d7-d5**

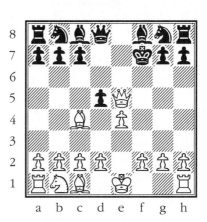

689. Not wishing to give up any of the extra material, even though it would clear the c8-bishop's diagonal for subsequent development, Black decides not to play 6...d7-d5 and instead plays the only other legal move: **6...Kf7-g6** (Diagram 191).

690. With the black king so exposed it's hard for White to go wrong. White chooses to drive the black king to the edge of the board by **7. Qe5-f5+** (Diagram 192), but White indeed has a follow-up in mind.

Diagram 190
**White would have played
7. Bc4xd5+**

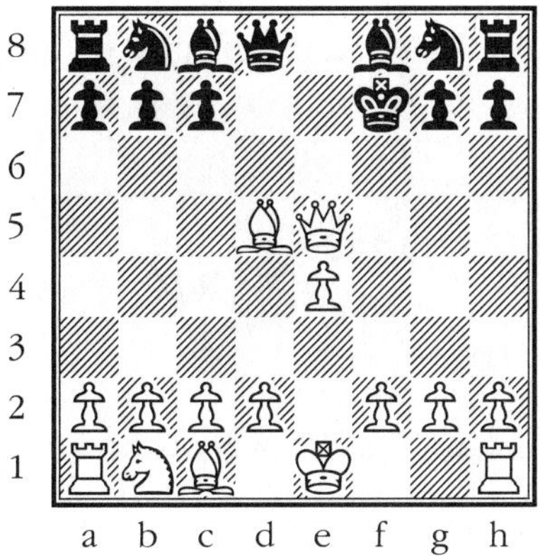

Diagram 191
After 6...Kf7-g6

Diagram 192
After 7. Qe5-f5+

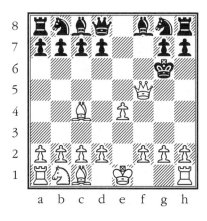

Diagram 193
After 7...Kg6-h6

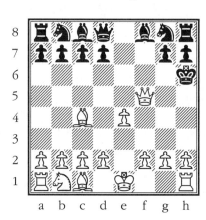

691. Since the white queen is protected by the pawn on e4, it can't be captured by the black king. Therefore Black has only one legal move: **7...Kg6-h6** (Diagram 193).

692. Once again White ignores a couple of reasonable queen checks (on f4 and h3) and instead brings a new piece to bear on the black king with **8. d2-d4+**. White's queen-bishop, without even moving, is now checking the king (Diagram 194).

Diagram 194
After 8. d2-d4+

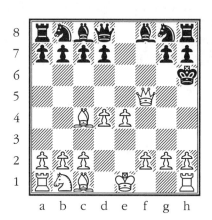

693. White's eighth move illustrates a kind of tactic not explained before: a discovered attack.

694. A **discovered attack** is a tactic by which one unit moves out of the way to uncover another friendly unit's line of attack.

695. The stationary unit gives the discovered attack.

696. When the moving unit also gives an attack the discovered attack is a double attack.

697. The most powerful form of discovered attack (the one that occurs in this game) is a **discovered check**.

698. A natural question here is how come White plays 8. d2-d4+ and not the safer 8. d2-d3+? Since both moves give discovered check, why advance two squares instead of one, since it doesn't really seem to matter?

699. There's no need to be so passive here and move the d-pawn merely one square. White's pressing an attack, and if you can assume control of the center with no extra effort, why not do so? But truly it's hardly relevant to the situation.

700. Black has two moves to get out of check, both of which rely on a block: with the queen (Qd8-g5) or with a pawn (g7-g5). Since Qd8-g5 allows mate in one move (Qf5xg5 mate), Black instead plays **8...g7-g5** (Diagram 195).

701. Now if White's c1-bishop takes the g5-pawn Black takes back with the queen (Qd8xg5). That line is fine, but White opts for a line that seems more promising. White sees that the g5-pawn is pinned to the black king by the c1-bishop. Thus the g5-pawn can't move.

702. Question: What should you try to do to a pinned enemy unit?

703. Answer: Attack it again, especially with a pawn. With that in mind White plays **9. h2-h4** (Diagram 196), at least threatening to fork the black king and queen by 10. Bc1xg5+.

Diagram 195
After 8...g7-g5

Diagram 196
After 9. h2-h4

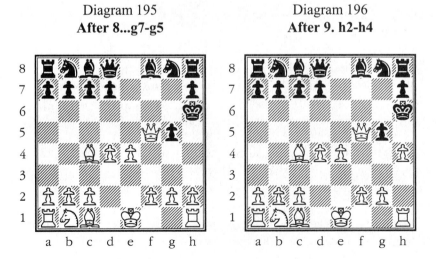

704. Here Black could play 9...Bf8-b4+ (Diagram 197), but White could easily then block the check with 10. c2-c3 (Diagram 198). That forces the black bishop to move again, so Black would simply be wasting time.

705. As a rule of thumb, steer clear of similar bishop checks, where the check can be blocked safely by a pawn, with the defender being able to "stick a pawn in the bishop's face." Such a check merely wastes time, since another move must then be wasted to save the suddenly threatened bishop.

706. Not every check is good. Don't give a check merely because it's check. (Don't pass bad checks.) Play a check simply because it's desirable as a move and not for other reasons extrinsic to what's happening on the board.

707. Instead of giving check Black protects the g5-pawn by **9...Bf8-e7** (Diagram 199).

708. Here White surprises Black, who expected 10. Bc1xg5+. Instead White plays **10. h4xg5+** (Diagram 200).

Diagram 197
**If Black had tried
9...Bf8-b4+**

Diagram 198
**White would have played
10. c2-c3**

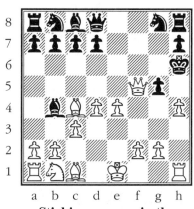

**Sticking a pawn in the
bishop's face**

709. This is no ordinary check, since Black is actually being checked twice: by the pawn and by the rook on h1. Therefore it's a double check, consisting of a direct check from a pawn and a discovered check from a rook.

710. Double check is a special form of discovered attack by which both the moving and stationary attackers give check.

Diagram 199
After 9...Bf8-e7

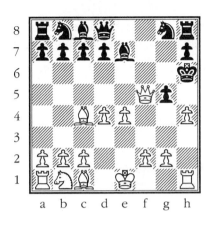

Diagram 200
After 10. h4xg5+

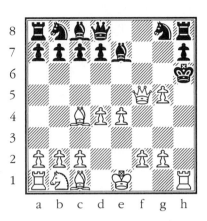

711. Since the only way to get out of double check is to move the king, Black does just that, making the sole legal response, **10...Kh6-g7** (Diagram 201).

712. Look very closely. See if you can find White's mate in one move.

713. It's mate with the queen, **11. Qf5-f7 mate** (Diagram 202).

714. To get more out of this game play it over one more time. But don't expect to memorize each move and each comment. It's just a game, and you'll probably never encounter the exact moves again. Instead try to un-

Diagram 201
After 10...Kh6-g7

Diagram 202
After 11. Qf5-f7 mate

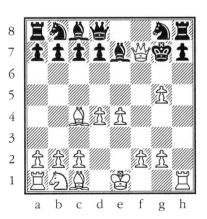

derstand the spirit of White's attack. Get a feel for the idea of sustained initiative and let it guide and inspire your own play.

715. In particular, note that White moved five different pieces and three different pawns. In the final position Black has only one developed piece (the dark-squared bishop).

716. Clearly, White didn't just attack Black: White's juggernaut overwhelmed Black.

717. Also notice that White didn't just check the black king pointlessly. Four of White's moves were checks that simultaneously brought out new pieces (the queen on move four, the two bishops on moves six and eight, and the rook on move ten).

718. After the opening mistakes Black seemed virtually helpless. From this game perhaps you see the virtue of aggressive play. It can give you the edge that ties up your opponent. After that it's a matter of playing off that growing initiative to fuel an irresistible assault against the enemy king.

719. There's a tendency to relax after getting a winning game. Most of us want our opponents to give up without a fight. But savvy veterans know better.

720. Wily defenders may even slow down the play, and that usually makes the superior side want to get it over with sooner. The result is the player with the edge unconsciously tends to move more quickly, without the quality of careful thought used to obtain the initial advantage. That typically enables the inferior side opportunities to get back in the game.

721. So the message is clear: after getting a winning advantage, work even harder at making sure you keep it – right down to mate.

Section Nineteen: More Chess Thinking

722. It's convenient to divide a chess game into three separate parts called **phases**. The three phases are:
   (a) the opening;
   (b) the middlegame;
   (c) the endgame.

723. There are no clear borders between the phases. Instead there are subtle changeovers that are often hard to perceive, even when they're taking place.

724. Each phase is described differently. The opening is the developing phase, the middlegame the strategic phase, the endgame the converting phase. These descriptions are largely true but not absolute.

725. For example, mistakes can be exploited in the opening and pieces can be developed in the endgame. However, it does seem that each phase has essentially its own character.

726. In the opening you gather the forces and prepare for action. In the middlegame you try to form a sound plan. In the endgame you use your advantages and minimize your weaknesses.

727. What might not be important in one phase may be significant suddenly in another.

728. For example, an extra pawn is not necessarily important in the opening but almost always important in the endgame.

729. Most endgames are decided by a pawn reaching the other side to become a new queen. A player with an extra queen is almost always able to force mate.

730. Sometimes both players try to push their pawns through to make new queens. In that case whoever makes a new queen first usually wins.

731. A wasted move in the endgame can be critical because it may allow the other player to make a new queen first.

732. Since king activity can also be crucial, wasting a move in the endgame might enable one king to gain a decisive placement over its counterpart.

733. Consequently the endgame has little to do with mate and much to do with pawn promotion.

734. In the endgame mate is rarely seen because most players resign after the other side makes a new queen. The chances of the inferior side winning after this are greatly reduced.

735. Mate happens far more frequently in the opening and middlegame, especially after one player makes a terrible mistake. In the endgame there usually aren't enough pieces left to exploit serious mistakes in the same way. Successful mating attacks usually need at least two pieces and a queen. But this doesn't mean that surprise checkmates don't occur in the endgame. They in fact often do, to one player's delight and the other's dismay.

736. Many players find endgame investigation too slow and uninteresting. Yet endgame study can have great practical value. Some of the game's greatest thinkers have made a case for learning endgame principles and basics fairly early on. They contend that such effort will pay off, perhaps not in the rapid improvement one sees by studying opening traps, which is often nothing more than showy flash, but eventually in definite and reliable gains in true playing strength. So when you get the chance, and you feel up to exploring it a bit, I suggest you try learning more about endgame principles, methods, and techniques. You might be happily surprised.

737. As implied, on the other hand, the opening is the easiest and most immediately practical phase to study because:
(a) you always start with the same position, so you can memorize it better;
(b) you get more practice with it, since every game must have an opening, but not necessarily a middlegame or endgame;
(c) you encounter two of the most important principles at once – centralization and development;
(d) you can win some games quickly, and this may inspire you to play more chess and learn it better.

738. The middlegame should also be considered early enough, especially middlegame tactics. But there are aspects to middlegame play which can be fairly hard to grasp, such as strategy and position play. To be sure, the middlegame stresses planning, logic, analysis, and reason – hallmarks of chess itself.

739. To play the middlegame well (or chess for that matter), you must know how to examine a chess position. Examining some middlegame positions can be quite difficult. (Who said life was easy?)

740. But even in a complicated middlegame, with unclear tactics and conflicting strategies abounding, you still can find a reasonable course of action.

741. The solution is to ask questions (in your head, of course). The right set of questions may enable you to gain insight into plausible options, and those refined possibilities can then help you formulate a rational plan.

742. In chess it can sometimes be better to have a bad plan than none at all. Though as a counter to that I am reminded of an old chess maxim: "If you don't know what to do, wait for your opponent to get an idea. It's bound to be wrong."

743. Regardless of a given position's complexity, certain types of questions in particular are more conducive to helping find a suitable plan.

744. But even before formulating a plan you have to get specific about something very important: your opponent's last move.

745. You can get focused on immediacies such as what your opponent just did with questions such as: Does my opponent's last move threaten me in any way? If so, can I deal with it? Are any of my units attacked? If so, are they protected enough times? Should I protect them further? Should I trade or move my attacked unit away? If I have to protect, can I do so with a pawn? (The best protection is often the least valuable unit available.)

746. After considering what your opponent is trying to do to you, you should get back to your own plans and consideration of your previous move. You might ask: Did I have a threat with my previous move? If so, did my opponent respond to it? If both of us have a threat, whose is more serious? Whose comes first? Can I ignore my opponent's move and go on with my own idea?

747. Now it's time to start merging these thoughts to take it further. You might ask: If I have to defend, can I threaten and defend at the same time? Can I find a move that negates my opponent's move and furthers my own previous move, adding to its impact? If no one is threatening anything can I threaten something? Can I do so while also improving my position? If I can't threaten can I at least improve my position, with the possibility of meaningfully threatening something after that?

748. The above types of questions are those that should be asked on your own time, when you're trying to consider your very next move. Under pressure to move you should stay with the most relevant areas of thought: threats and counterthreats.

749. But on your opponent's time, when your opponent is on the move, you're not as pressed and can think a little differently. That's when you can ask questions of a more general nature to unearth useful information.

750. The chief thing to do when you're not so pressed is to assess who stands better and why. It's only after you understand what's what that you can decide on a plan relevant to your circumstances.

751. At this point, when you're not so pressured, you should seek all kinds of general information. You'll want to know whose ahead in material, if anyone is. If you're ahead, it's likely you'll want to trade pieces and head toward a manageable endgame. If you're behind, you'll want to avoid trades and complicate the position.

752. But there are all sorts of other considerations to be made too. Who has more space? Who has the initiative? Whose pawn structure is better? Whose king is safer? And so on. To appreciate these concerns and the questions they raise you'll need to turn to another book, and possibly other books after that.

753. To be sure, the process of asking questions could go on and on, like Hegelian dialectic, thesis, antithesis and synthesis to perpetuity. Don't go there.

754. Instead, when you feel the time is right in a given chess position, ask just one question: What would I like to do if I could?

755. This is a remarkable question. It's not profound, but it gets right to the heart of the matter.

756. In some cases it will immediately direct you to a good idea and you'll be able to take advantage of it.

757. Most of the time it won't give you anything like your next move. You'll be surprised, though, how often it may steer you in a desirable and pertinent direction.

758. For example, a possible internal monologue, surely expressed in your own words, might go like this: Oh yeah, I'd like to do that. But I can't. Yet it does seem quite nice. Okay, how can I play it to maximize the chance of that being done? Or some reckoning like that.

759. The key thing is that a progression of relevancy is started. You may not be able to do everything you'd like, but the process ensures at least getting to a plan that's more relevant than a randomly chosen one, based perhaps on the very first move that pops into your head.

760. No matter how you get there – that is, to the end of your analysis – you'll have come to your intended next move. Don't yet play it.

761. Instead, ask one final question, just to make sure you haven't missed anything.

762. Ask something like: Does my opponent have a check, capture, or serious threat that, if played, could overturn my analysis?

763. The mere asking of this question, or some question comparable to it, brings it all back into focus. It may save you from making a terrible mistake.

764. Questions in general, however they're posed, have a particular end result in mind: to impose pertinence and order on your thinking. Indeed, the give-and-take of intelligent questioning has a way of introducing a self-organizing structure over the entire enterprise.

765. Better organization tends to produce better thinking.

766. You're not expected to ask or answer all or any of the relevant questions completely or conclusively. But by trying to pose them and others like them you may become more aware of different possibilities and solutions. Ask the right questions and you have the directional cues needed to find a suitable plan.

767. The process of asking questions to determine a course of action is known as **the analytic method**.

768. The analytic method doesn't work as well if you don't ask good questions, and it's hard to exploit what you can't express. So whenever feasible get into the habit of trying to translate your chess ideas into words everyone could understand, since that's the best way for *you* to understand. Alexander Kotov, a famous Russian grandmaster and teacher, once said that if we can't put our thoughts into words, they probably don't exist. If they don't exist, do we? That's enough Cartesian mischief for now.

Section Twenty: Conclusion

769. You've probably grasped some points and possibly misunderstood others in the course of learning how to play chess. This is natural in the study of any subject. Chess, of course, is not any old subject. It's a game of skill, and it's also a game of strategy.

770. A strategy game is one that requires making decisions with imperfect information, often in the teeth of profound uncertainty.

771. But chess is actually a game of perfect information, since everything exists right before both participants. That is, there's no hidden information, as in certain card games.

772. But therein is a paradox. Although chess has no hidden information, the options are so great that it's ridiculously impossible for the human mind to see all that the game camouflages.

773. So in a very practical sense you must strategize to get through the myriad contingencies, hidden or not. To that end there's a need to make sophisticated generalizations based on whatever sensible information can be discerned.

774. This is where principles become useful. They can cut through many of the veils of disguise you'd like to see through and possibly haven't.

775. After trying to comprehend the mysteries of a given position you can take those suggested guidelines and, supported by analysis and concrete variations, try to come up with a suitable plan.

776. Generally, you'll want to strive for as much as you can get while incurring as little risk as possible. To that end it's often joked that grandmasters don't play to win. Nor do they play for a draw. Rather they play not to lose, living close to the edge but making sure not to fall off it.

777. There are two basic strategies in chess: to simplify or to complicate. Between those two transactional states are a range of possibilities swinging one way or the other.

778. As a reminder, you simplify by exchanging off pieces, avoiding problematical lines, and taking no undue chances. With this approach you try to keep control of the position.

779. You complicate by shunning trades, seeking intricacy, and taking calculated risks. With this approach you hope to confuse your opponent and gain control of the position.

780. But in every case, winning or losing, ahead or behind, you're still trying to play reasonably within the context of sound principles.

781. Underlying your methodology should be the understanding that there's always a best strategy, and your job is to find or approximate it.

782. To be sure, the only time you're justified in taking unsound chances is when you have a hopelessly lost position. In that case, since you're lost, you have nothing to lose. Or as my teacher used to say to me, a dying man can eat anything.

783. At the start of a chess game the position is in a state of dynamic equilibrium. At least in theory, whatever you can do can be counterbalanced by your opponent.

784. Theoretically this suggests (though it doesn't prove) that a game of chess should end in a draw.

785. If this is true, that a game of chess is hypothetically drawn, what strategy should one employ to increase the possibility of obtaining a winning game?

786. The answer worked out by Wilhelm Steinitz, the first world chess champion (1886-1894), is to play for small advantages.

787. These advantages could be so small and apparently inconsequential that the opponent doesn't see them or dismisses them.

788. None of these advantages individually may imply much. But taken together these miniscule plusses can become irresistibly bound to a winning attack.

789. To break that attack the defender may have to surrender something concrete, such as a pawn or minor piece.

790. Theoretically, the position then falls back to an equilibrating state, with one crucial difference: the attacker has essentially "stolen" something from the opponent. And what is it he or she has stolen? Probably it's an amount of material (piece, pawn, or whatever) which had to be surrendered to break the attacker's growing initiative.

791. This overall approach falls under the umbrella of **positional chess**. It's what strong players generally do: they accumulate small, often intangible advantages and convert that admixture into a winning game.

792. But this is not necessarily easy stuff, and you'll come to understand it better after you've read other books, played many games, and generally thought much more about chess.

793. And that's what you have to do next: start playing more chess.

794. If you studied the violin, but never played, do you think you'd be a good violin player? Probably not (just a guess).

795. Play chess with friends and make new friends who play chess. Join a chess club if your neighborhood has one. Either your local library or the nearest school, university, or social organization should be able to tell you if a club exists. Each may have a chess club.

796. Play chess on the Internet. The ICC is a good place to start, though there are other wonderful sites as well. I'd also check out the online services of the USCF and the *ChessCafe.com*. Both are excellent and should prove to be very helpful.

797. But as you play and explore this wonderful game don't despair if improvement seems to be lagging. Chess growth is almost quantum in nature. You can be playing and studying for a long time yet it seems you're still not getting anywhere.

798. Suddenly it all comes together. Almost mysteriously you seem to jump to the next level and you can't quite explain it. Actually, you've probably been getting more adept with every game and new insight. It just doesn't translate into tangible gain until everything falls into place.

799. Only direct experience can put everything in place – lots of it and the best kind. You've taken what I hope has been a pleasant and informative first play on what should remain an enduring voyage of stimulation, challenge, art and beauty. Your next move lies ahead, and that should be to begin enjoying regular chess in the company of challenging opposition. Good luck in all of those encounters and on the rest of your lifelong passage.

800. I hope I've at least answered some of your questions. If I had a final question, I think it would be about where, when, and how to start that journey. The answer I'd like to get would be here, now, and with a consuming passion.

General Index